D0952425

Praise for *Covert Persuasion*

"This blockbuster book blows the doors off of many of the persuasion myths that are passed around carelessly by gurus who haven't really done the research. It's about time someone dealt you a persuasion hand from a deck without any jokers. If you are at all curious about persuasion, this book is absolutely essential."

—Mark Joyner, best-selling author
of *The Great Formula*

"*Covert Persuasion* is like Grandmom's secret recipe: priceless and so delicious. Every tip and persuasion tactic is a tasty morsel that will leave you stuffed and still craving more. The only difference is Grandmom won't tell you her secret, but Hogan and Speakman reveal every secret ingredient that you need to bring out the master persuader in you."

—Al "The Inspiration" Duncan,
professional speaker and co-author
of *Unleash the Greatness Within You*

"When you absolutely, positively need a 'yes,' *Covert Persuasion* reveals the tools to manufacture their compliance. It is better to read this book and never use this revelatory technology than to need these techniques and find yourself stupid. You are complicit to the extent you don't know how you're being manipulated. Congratulations on inquiring into this power. Now, buy this book and use the force for good."

—Ben Mack, author of the upcoming
Think Two Products Ahead

"As a multiple business owner in the service industry, I highly value anything written by Dr. Hogan about the art of persuasion. Time and again, I have been able to successfully navigate tough business and legal negotiations using the knowledge and techniques I've learned through Dr. Hogan's courses and books and consider his materials my 'business persuasion bible'! I now have a respectable library of Dr. Hogan's material that I and my staff continually reference, and I am more than excited to add his latest book, *Covert Persuasion*, to my collection. In fact, Dr. Hogan's material is required reading for any new member of my business team. I won't do business without him!"

—Michelle Drum Matteson, President of
The Razorz Edge, Charleston, Illinois

"*Covert Persuasion* is founded in solid research. And its how-to-do-it approach should more than satisfy any who want to persuade ethically and very effectively."

—Phil Hamilton, President of Hamilton
Business Group, Austin, Texas

"Hogan and Speakman have collected a lot of valuable wisdom that's second nature to the best salespeople in the world. It's a handbook for the rest of us."

—Martha Rogers, Ph.D., founder of Peppers
and Rogers Group and co-author of *Return
on Customer: Creating Maximum Value from
Your Scarcest Resource*

COVERT PERSUASION

Psychological Tactics and Tricks to Win the Game

KEVIN HOGAN
JAMES SPEAKMAN

WILEY

John Wiley & Sons, Inc.

Published by John Wiley & Sons, Inc., Hoboken, New Jersey.
Published simultaneously in Canada.

For general information on our other products and services or for technical support please contact our Customer Care Department within the United States at (800) 762-2974, outside the United States at (317) 572-3993 or fax (317) 572-4002.

Wiley also publishes its books in a variety of electronic formats. Some content that appears in print may not be available in electronic books. For more information about Wiley products, visit our web site at www.wiley.com.

Library of Congress Cataloging-in-Publication Data:

Hogan, Kevin.
    Covert persuasion : psychological tactics and tricks to win the game /
Kevin Hogan, James Speakman.
        p.   cm.
    Includes bibliographical references and index.
    ISBN-13: 978-0-470-05141-2 (cloth : alk. paper)
    ISBN-10: 0-470-05141-8 (cloth : alk. paper)
        1. Persuasion (Psychology).   2. Selling—Psychological aspects.   3.
Interpersonal communication.   4. Interpersonal relations.   I. Speakman,
James, 1968–   II. Title.
    BF637.P4H63   2006
    153.8'52—dc22
                                                                2006011009

Printed in the United States of America.

10   9   8   7   6   5

For
Katie, Jessica, and Mark
—Kevin

For
Maria
—James

Contents

Acknowledgments

I (KH) thank our editor, Matt Holt, for making this project a reality. There are always a lot of people who inspire your work . . . or help keep you sane while you work! Scott and Carmen Schluter, Devin and Rachel Hastings, Meredith Kaplan, Ron Stubbs, Michelle Drum, Tonya Reiman, Todd Bramson, Jan Snyder, Cheryl Boldon.

I (JS) would also like to thank our editor, Matt Holt, and Kevin Hogan for the opportunity to work together on this book; Laura Kidder Dickerhoof for all her hard work, proofreading and editing; Mom and Dad for always supporting my efforts in every direction; Laura Speakman for all her help; Ray Hexamer for being a good friend and mentor; Brian Tracy for his encouragement.

Introduction

How do you persuade another person to buy or try your product or service, contribute to your cause, or vote for your candidate? The answer is in this book. *Covert Persuasion* is a meticulously researched book that synthesizes diverse sources of study and then draws new conclusions that will help you to persuade others more consistently and more effectively.

Covert Persuasion. The title alone draws up images of the clandestine and secretive. And obviously, that's what our goal was for this book. Our first goal is to show you techniques and strategies to persuade others with such skill that your efforts are literally not observable. They are covert. Using the powers of Covert Persuasion in your personal and business life is not only ethical and correct, but also necessary to your overall success.

Much of *Covert Persuasion* deals with the accurate prediction of human behavior in any given context.

Throughout history there have been literally hundreds, if not thousands, of attempts to categorize people in an effort to better understand them and predict their behavior. A quick history of this effort reveals several of the most legendary names in psychology, philosophy, Neuro-Linguistic Programming (NLP), consumer behavior, and business. From the days of Plato, Freud, Jung, B.F. Skinner,

Carl Rogers, William James, and Abraham Maslow to the more contemporary minds in psychology, business, and advertising; these great minds and others have come up with some amazing ways to try and explain our collective thinking and decision-making in order to persuade us and control and direct our behavior.

Some examples of attempts to categorize all of us include the Myers Briggs Type Indicator, the Hermann Brain Dominance Indicator, and the Language and Behavioral Profile. There are, of course, the countless personality tests that try to determine if you are well suited to a career in sales. In addition to these, there is the personality Enneagram and, of course, the standard 4-quadrant description of us as a Thinker, Relater, Socializer, or Director.

We also have the popular theory that all our behavior stems from our desire to avoid pain and seek pleasure. Can it be as simple as that? We'll discuss that in the pages ahead.

There's also the entire field of language research where it is believed that the words you use determine the feelings you experience. Your emotions are dictated by the labels (words) you place on the experiences you have. This research has a great history beginning in the 1950s and has remained a powerful set of principles to use as a guide as you go forward to persuade others to your way of thinking. But even this theory, as helpful as it is in some contexts, is fraught with errant thinking when analyzing others.

> Everything you now have or ever will have, become, do, or experience, you will get with and through other people. Life IS persuasion!

The world is the ultimate context for Persuasion. Marketers and advertisers are making literally countless attempts to understand each and every one of us more clearly. They will spend hundreds of millions of dollars each year trying to grab our attention, persuade us to buy their product or service, sample their offering, vote for their candidate, and/or contribute to their cause. In fact, if you live in the United States you alone, are the recipient of over $3,200 of marketing and advertising messages each year. That's a lot of money spent to persuade you.

In this book, we have captured a giant list of Covert Persuasion techniques. Starting inside your own head with the self-talk that is necessary for the confidence required to influence others, all the way to the final act of communicating directly with the person you want to persuade, your *target person*, it's all here. We've researched all the techniques for you.

We believe that what you read here will ignite a passion for learning more about this fascinating subject. To help you in that never ending search for more knowledge, we've included a comprehensive bibliography at the end of this book.

Drawing from a wide cross section of persuasion research including experiments in social psychology, neurolinguistic programming, language research, creative thinking, sales techniques, business communication skills, and personal communication skills, you're going to find startling new insights that will change the way you communicate forever.

We've included information to help you understand the other person. We'll also cover the power of questions to persuade the other person's thinking and behavior as well.

Our goal is to have your persuasion skills primed to an expert level so that you get more of what you want, when you want it. If you're in sales, you will now have tools at your disposal that will, when you actively and consistently put the ideas and techniques to work every day in your working life, double or even triple your sales and commissions. It sounds wild but you won't be in the first 1,000 to tell us that this is what transpired.

If you're in business and you need to convince co-workers, subordinates, and/or supervisors to go along with your ideas, keep reading. You'll find a lot of techniques here that you can use immediately to covertly persuade others to your way of thinking.

This book will become a dog-eared resource guide to help you stay focused on exactly what you want while providing you with a quick, but very powerful, collection of proven persuasion techniques.

Few people know how to look for the motivational drivers of behavior. Yet they determine what you and I do. Using the unique covert observation and subtle questioning techniques you'll find only in this book, you'll have a very high degree of success reading the other person. From that point, you'll use the persuasion techniques in this book to direct their thinking and behavior toward the goals that you want accomplished.

In addition, we'll cover the words that are more persuasive than any others when it comes to your personal and business life. These words combined in powerful stories will help you to persuade more people, more often.

Warning

The persuasion techniques in this book are designed to be used ethically. Just like a hammer is designed to drive a nail into wood, but can be misused to hit someone in the head, so these techniques are designed to increase your persuasive power for good in both your professional and personal life, and not for evil or unethical purposes.

The techniques in this book are often presented in a blunt, straightforward fashion, so you will easily be able to learn to bring someone else to your way of thinking. All of this happens in a very short amount of time with as little resistance as possible to accomplish *your* goals.

Oh! I almost forgot. A bonus for you! Throughout the book, there are *$10,000 Covert Persuasion Tricks*. These are very specific things that you can do to increase your effectiveness at persuading the other person. If done with maximum skill, the trick can easily yield $10,000 or more in increased sales, profits, or savings. Or, if your specific desired outcome is not literally measurable in dollars, using one of the *$10,000 Covert Persuasion Tricks* may yield a result that is certainly worth a great deal in terms of feelings, emotions, and the things you can't put a price on.

That's a lot to cover in one book—and it's all for you!

Let's get started!

1 | Covert Persuasion Begins in the Mind

There are millions of words written about how the human brain works and about as many different opinions and theories about exactly how we think. However, one thing is for sure. In order to persuade someone else to your way of thinking, you must align your mind with theirs. Successful persuasion begins and ends when there is a "mind meld" of real meaning, feeling, and understanding.

So how do we establish this mind meld? How do we consistently become more adept at persuading other people to our way of thinking? The answer lies in understanding what motivates and drives the other person. Armed with that knowledge, you can position your thoughts and requests in such a way that they are easily and quickly accepted by other persons with little or no questioning. *They'll see you as very much like them and feel compelled to comply with your requests.*

Before we get started, let's take a look at a couple of quick definitions of exactly what "Covert" and "Persuasion" really mean. There is a lot to be learned in the understanding of the combination of these two powerful words. Let's look at what each one means.

2

Covert *(adj.)* Concealed, hidden, secret

Persuade *(n.)* to cause (someone) to do something by means of argument, reasoning, or entreaty. (2) To win over (someone) to a course of action by reasoning or inducement. (3) To make (someone) believe something; convince

Persuasion *(n.)* the act of persuading

By definition then, things that are *covert* are not out in plain sight. They are kept from easy view, concealed, and hidden. When we combine this with the act of convincing someone of something we end up with our effort of persuasion not being noticed by the target person(s).

For the purpose of this book, *Covert Persuasion* is about bypassing the critical factor of the human mind without the process being known to the receiver of the message. It's about getting past both resistance and reactance. This is accomplished when one person sends a message and the message is received without significant critical thought or questioning on the part of the receiver.

Sometimes Covert Persuasion is about "state" manipulation and management. What is the other person's state of mind? That's the question you'll be able to answer after reading this book.

In the environment of selling, for example, the person does not have to buy the product or service; actually, buying is not a sign that Covert Persuasion has taken place. A person without money could easily have been persuaded and placed in a buying state, but he simply didn't have the money.

A Word about Ethics

Many people ask us if it is ethical to "persuade" someone to do something. The easy answer is absolutely *yes*. Not only is it ethical but it's necessary. Our economy (and our family and our business) function because of the fact that people are being persuaded to buy, try, vote, make their bed, shut the door, and contribute. Millions of communication messages are wittingly or unwittingly exchanged every single day. These are all designed to cause you and me to take some kind of action.

Ethics, however, really rest with the person who is attempting to persuade another. In the research we have done, we have uncovered and developed several hundred specific persuasion techniques. All of these are powerful. When used ethically and responsibly, they advance everyone's position.

The Power of Suggestion Changes Perception

Covert Persuasion is, in part, about creating change in the mind of your clients or customers without them necessarily being aware of the changes that are occurring.

One of the most powerful tools to begin this change in your customer's mind is using the right words. At the right time, the right words can change minds and lives.

The Right Words in a Question Form Can Direct Thinking

In an experiment done in the 1970s by Elizabeth Loftus (one of the world's leading memory researchers), people viewed slides of a pedestrian-auto accident. They were shown a slide of a red Datsun (a sporty little car) at a yellow Yield sign. The group was asked, "Did you see another car pass the Datsun at the stop sign?" When asked, most of the group remembered a Stop sign instead of a Yield sign. The verbal information, the words, and the question by the researcher altered the memory of what they had seen.

Covert Persuasion. That's one snapshot.

COVERT PERSUASION TRICK

A suggestion from an authority figure can often override a person's visual memory to create a new and different memory. That means people will think different things depending on who is doing the telling. Imagine what would happen if you used quotes around your client's authority figure's words as you and he talk. "I know how much you like Bono. Well, he said . . ." And magic happens.

Our objective with Covert Persuasion is to create images in the customer's mind that target the behavior we want (to buy, try, contribute, vote, etc). Using the correct and most powerful word combinations mixed with the right questions leads to directed thinking and, ultimately, the action of the customer toward the goals we want accomplished.

When Resistance Is Likely, Distraction Creates a Receptive and Easily Persuaded Mind

Because we naturally resist what we don't believe and we experience reactance to all that we fear, there is a real need to help customers create new pictures with new information to allow them to arrive at a new outcome in their head. This new outcome will be favorable to you and the ultimate sale of your product or service because you helped the customer create the new picture of what the future will look like.

Funny thing is that before you paint those pictures you want to address the resistance. Whatever it is that is causing the resistance or reactance (unconscious level resistance), you typically want to address it. In fact, for the most part, if you don't preclude it, you must address it.

People are quickly receptive to information and attitudes that agree with their point of view. People will formulate arguments on the spot against any point of view that disagrees with their currently held belief. Always discover current beliefs and attitudes so you can affirm them in some way. On the other hand, *do not have your customer verbally state anything that you will want him to change later. Once an attitude is communicated (verbally or in writing) it will be maintained, even in the face of overwhelming evidence to the contrary.*

COVERT PERSUASION TRICK

Resistance is diminished when people agree with the presented point of view.

Affirm the individual's point of view.

Eight Steps to Get Your Outcome

There are a number of models (clusters of tactics that make up a strategy) for utilizing Covert Persuasion. Here's the first.

1. *Identify a targeted problem/situation.* This is the thing your target no longer wants to experience. It could be high costs, high employee turnover, inventory spoilage, ineffective advertising, almost anything that's not going right (and that your product or service is well suited to solve).

2. *Help your customer see that continuing with this problem/situation without addressing it will ultimately cost him/her in many painful ways.* There is powerful psychology behind this tactic. Trigger the pain button first, before even beginning to talk about

possible solutions or how you, your product, or your service can help.

3. *Have your customers/clients identify a preferred outcome.* It is critical to have *them* choose a better outcome. Sometimes this is prompted by a simple question from you like: "What would you rather have happen?" or "What would be better than that?" or "What would be a perfect outcome for you?"

4. *Have your customers identify the consequences of this new outcome.* This is very important in helping them accept the new outcome. This step is also prompted by questions that you will ask. It's often as simple as: "What would this new outcome mean for you and your company?" When they answer they are forming a new thought direction that will lead them to your product or service.

5. *Confirm that this new chosen outcome is what they really want.* Sometimes clients/customers will tell you what they think *you* want to hear. This doesn't help anyone. They must tell the truth. They have to be honest with themselves, and with you, for real solid behavior to follow (saying "yes" to cooperating with you and all the actions that involves).

6. *You need to be certain the new outcome is truly going to be good for your customer/client.* It does no long-term good for your reputation or your company's reputation to do a quick short-term, bad-fit sale. No, you want the customer to truly benefit from all the features of your product or service. So, make sure the fit is genuine and true.

7. *Do not judge.* If you perceive a response by a customer or client to be inappropriate don't be too quick to judge it. He might have a different point of view than you do as you both initially meet. Take some time to understand and relate to clients. Once you do this, their response may seem to make

more sense and you might find they are resonating 100 percent with your message.

8. *Never tell your target person he is wrong.* This is a restatement of that old saying, "The customer is always right!" That may not always be true, but it's a good caution sign in your own mind. When you think about it, how would you feel if someone told you that you were wrong? You would probably get defensive and try to show or prove that you were in fact right. You would end up clinging more tightly to that position. Your customers will react the exact same way. Never tell them they are wrong or that buying your competitors' product last year was a mistake. Your customers will immediately wonder if buying from you would be a mistake.

2 | From "No" to "Yes"

**The Most Common Reason Your Target Says "No"
and How to Overcome It**

The reason that word "no" comes out of people's mouths is because it is an *instant reaction*. They did this or something like this before and they determined quickly it was a bad decision. About 90 percent of all "No's" come from this background.

Now pay close attention.

COVERT PERSUASION FACT

"No" is an instant reaction and doesn't mean anything. People don't know why they say "no." They don't know why they do what they do; especially in retrospect and they will perform opposite behaviors depending on the words you use in each communication you have. In other words, people are utterly out of control . . . until the Covert Persuasion Expert walks in the door.

Imagine you're enjoying a shower. All of a sudden the water turns cold. You turn around in the shower and quickly turn the temperature up up up. But it doesn't go up. Someone else is using the hot water in the house! You turn it off instantly. That relaxing 20-minute shower has been destroyed. Six months later you still remember the episode as someone being incredibly rude and that it was a bad shower. You absolutely don't remember the previous 20 minutes of relaxation.

The next day you take a five-minute shower. It feels good. Warm, relaxing. But you remember that someone will probably start using the hot water so you get out fairly quickly, and it was a nice shower. Relaxing, if short. And later that week, you remember that it was a good shower.

All relationships have ups and downs. Most of the time they are in the middle. Much of your time is spent working, cleaning the house. You are not focusing on the relationship with your housemate. Then you go through a period where the two of you argue, fight, and bicker. Ugh. It's horrible! Time for a new relationship. The news is broken. Arguments escalate. You knew it! And for the rest of your life you tell people that you can't believe you stuck with that relationship for 25 years.

In order to understand how to influence others you need to understand how people make decisions, how they remember the past, and how they see the future. This is what has been missing for many and what makes persuasion a "numbers game" for most.

As you've seen from the above examples:

1. People remember *peak* experiences, especially the really bad ones.

2. They certainly remember how things *end*.

COVERT PERSUASION TRICK

People remember peak experiences (especially the bad ones) and how things end.

When asking about your competitor, elicit the peak experiences and the customer's last experience. (They wouldn't be seeing you if they were totally satisfied.)

When changing your customer's state of mind (if necessary), have him bring you to peak experiences and remember the last time he bought something that was a brilliant purchase.

---

3. People do not see the future clearly. They do not know how they will feel when certain events come to pass, even if they're looking forward to them.

You will see that all of this is crucial in communication, persuasion, and obviously your business and relationships.

COVERT PERSUASION TACTIC

People experience fear because they don't see the future clearly. It's ambiguous. It's scary. It's NO . . . *until you bring them out there safely!*

In fact, this might be some of the most important information you have ever learned.

Have you ever been in a conversation with someone and then that person says, "Why did you say that?"

"I didn't say that!"

"Yes, you did, I heard you!"

"I did not!"

That night in separate conversations (or journal entries) both of you make the other person out to be an idiot or thoughtless or something else that isn't positive.

Clearly one of you is incorrect, but both of you are equally certain that your memory is correct. The fact is that trying to resolve this is impossible. This is the problem of memory. The brain makes stuff up out of thin air to fill in blank spots. Everyone experiences these moments where they said or heard (or *saw*!) something that actually wasn't articulated or heard. You can't convince a brain otherwise because, it was there!

Now, if you can't rely on memory to know what really happened 30 seconds ago, how can you rely on it for accurately representing what happened in the past? Answer: You can't but only you know this. You know this if you read *Coffee with Kevin Hogan*, the must-have e-zine that comes every week in your e-mailbox. (Subscribe at www.kevinhogan.com.) The other person doesn't read *Coffee*! Therefore you have to either move past this point or give him a short course in neuroscience. You can start with this:

In one recent research study, people were having a necessary colonoscopy. During the process they were asked to report their level of discomfort at regular intervals. At the end of the process for one group the scope was allowed to simply "not move" for a minute right before it was removed. The other group had the scopes removed a minute earlier (when the colonoscopy was actually finished) and with no additional minute of rest.

Results: The group who had the scope in longer but finished easier remember the colonoscopy very differently from those who had the shorter time colonoscopy. The colonoscopy group that had the extra minute of no scope movement while still inserted, remembered the colonoscopy as "not that bad." The group that had no extra moments of rest remembered it as much worse.

COVERT PERSUASION TRICK

Key point: When matched with how people actually reported they felt at each interval in the moment (not later that night in a journal entry), memory reflected the *end of the memory* and not the entire experience. *People remember how it finished and generalize it back to the rest of the experience.*

Strategy: At each step, know that the person you are talking with does not operate with a video camera in his mind. He operates on his memories. It doesn't matter if they are accurate or not. Therefore you need to clearly show how not acting (in a way he recalls as being painful in the past) will have dire consequences.

Do: Then you must show how both decisions could play out along with the probabilities of both.

For people who lost money in the stock market, you can understand their interest in staying in the money market. Unfortunately, the reality is that they are probably going to go broke if they do that. You simply can't tell them to ignore the past. You must point out that it *could* happen again, though it is more likely that because the environment is not completely different, typical results are more likely.

The research in persuasion is clear. You *must* point out *both possible futures* for you to be successful. Otherwise, the person will be destined to go with what he feels instead of what makes sense. The phobia of losing is tough to get past without at least acknowledging and examining those possible outcomes.

Then finish with a very clear picture of a very likely future. If you paint it too rosy, you will both lose. The other person will feel manipulated. If you paint it realistically, there is an excellent chance that he will respond appropriately.

Ultimately the stock market crashed, the Titanic sank, the Twin Towers went down, but that is not a reason to avoid the stock market, boating, or tall buildings. In fact, having failed in the first two quarters of the game is all the more reason to try harder in the second half.

That is the message that needs to be made clear to your clients, and they will get it if you use that metaphor. Never let a bad result in the past turn your client into a non-client.

Introducing Omega Strategies

Knowles, Crawford, and Linn might sound like a legal team but they are a group of professors at the University of Arkansas, and for the past several years they have done more research into reducing resistance than anyone I know. Their work has influenced mine greatly. Reducing resistance is accomplished with what the good doctors call "Omega Strategies." An Omega Strategy is a persuasion strategy that does not try to improve or enhance the value of the product, but is solely focused on reducing reactance and resistance in the process of persuasion.

To know that reciprocity is effective is one thing. To know how and when to induce reciprocity is quite another. To know that asking for a favor can be a powerful technique of influence is different from knowing when to ask, and how. I want to show you how to communicate persuasively using a couple of separate techniques of influence, and I also want to show you what not to do.

"Son, if you do that you will kill yourself," said Mom, and the son went right back to doing it again—remember?

Mom neglected a key factor of influence that almost everyone forgets. Make a note.

$10,000 COVERT PERSUASION TACTIC

Give specific instructions or steps when directing or attempting to influence behavior. Simply telling someone to stop doing something or to "get a job" or "behave" or "shut up" is utterly and completely destined to fail because these are not instructions.

Decades of research reveal that specific instructions are necessary to influence and induce compliance. What does this mean to you? It means that you need to walk people step by step through a process that leads them to the door you ultimately want them to open. Anything short of doing this is unlikely to succeed in the short or long term.

I could detail all of the research and go in-depth here but I'll save that for the newly available Science of Influence CD program now available at www.kevinhogan.com. Instead I want to direct your attention (*did you catch that?*) to another technique that can be remarkably influential or explode in your face: fear.

Fear is something we are all wired to fight or flee from. Our irrational fears are those that we attempt to conquer and overcome. No one likes to experience fear. Fear literally can motivate people in ways few other things can.

"If you have sex without a condom you could get AIDS!" That statement could induce fear or not. It could induce a behavioral change but it probably won't. The word "AIDS" now is a bit like "accident." The public has been inoculated to the word through overuse.

"Imagine that you keep smoking those cigarettes and what you see is your kids and your grandkids coming to look at you in your casket, crying because they can't speak with you anymore because you committed a slow suicide with tobacco. Your face is shriveled and they will never think of you in the same way."

That is a scary scenario for most people with children. (You've used fear in a powerful fashion.) Let's follow it up with, "And if you cut to half of a pack of cigarettes each day this month and to a cigarette each day next month and finally throw the pack away, wouldn't it be something to see you healthy and happy, having fun playing with those grandkids?"

What happened here? We scared the hell out of our friend and then we gave him a specific set of instructions to follow. That's persuasive. However, in the case of cigarette smokers they may have heard it 50,000 times, in which case they are vaccinated against your proposal and they will not pay attention to your petition. Once a person has heard the same words or concepts over and over the words become impotent. What to do?

And is it ethical? That's an interesting question and books have been written about such things. I don't know the answer to the question but I'm glad we brought it up. A good rule of thumb is to always act in the very best interests of everyone you communicate with.

The lesson here is simple. If you are going to use fear in a communication in order to foster change or alter behavior or encourage someone to buy your product, idea, or service, you must also include a step-by-step set of instructions in your message in order for it to be successful.

The First Covert Formula for Change:
Negative Emotions + Behavioral Plan ==> Behavioral Change

What happens when *two* scary or anxiety producing experiences compete with each other for the person's behavioral response? Academic researchers have been studying *anticipated regret* for the last few years and here is a scenario that was proposed to 164 UCLA students.

You've parked your car in the lot and you are rushing to class for an important quiz you don't want to be late for. You realize on the way that you may have left your car unlocked.

Half of the students were then told to imagine how they would feel if they go back to the car, find it was locked all along, and now they have missed the quiz. The other half of the students were then told to imagine how they would feel if they didn't go back to the car, took the quiz, only to come back to the car and discover it had been vandalized. How would they feel then?

All students were then asked whether they would go back to the car or go to take the quiz. Of those told to imagine the car vandalized, 69 percent said they would return to the car and check to see if the doors were locked. Those who were told they would miss the quiz? 34.5 percent said they'd go back and check on the car. A control group showed 46 percent returning to check on the car.

Lesson: In general, where the students experienced anticipated regret, they said they would take the action appropriate to prevent the regret from happening.

We all know that what people say they will do and what they actually do in real life are very different things. Later research has in fact validated this fact. Where people experience anticipated regret, they tend to take action to prevent the regret. As people of influence, that's a mighty important thing to remember.

Covert Power Project

Write down 10 things you can do in your business where if people don't take advantage of your product or service, these negative things will happen to them. In other words, how can you take advantage of the concept of anticipated regret?

Covert Persuasion: Changing Beliefs

Beliefs stick like super glue in the brain when you are attempting to persuade someone who believes something that runs counter to your proposal.

You want your clients to buy you, your product, and your service. They have a belief about you, your product, and your service. You want to change it and have proof beyond a shadow of a doubt that their belief is wrong and that evidence you have is correct. They will not buy from you if you show them that evidence, even if it is crystal-clear proof. You face an uphill (though not impossible) battle.

How uphill? You already know that people stick with political parties and religions (the reason you aren't supposed to talk about them in polite conversation) regardless of evidence to the contrary.

I remember when the California campaign to elect Bob Dole president asked for my assistance in 1996. I said no. Part of the platform at the time in the Republican Party was that cigarettes aren't that bad for you. (I'm paraphrasing to keep this short.) How idiotic can you get? But tobacco was putting big money into the Dole campaign. They therefore were downplaying the negative effects of tobacco and I wasn't interested in being associated with anything like that. (I happen to like Bob Dole very much, by the way; this was simply crossing an ethical boundary in my mind.)

My belief was strong that promoting the idea that tobacco is less deadly than it is would simply be wrong. I would never be able to live with myself. It took almost 10 seconds to make this decision.

Political and religious beliefs run deep because of the degree that they are defended against others who believe otherwise. The more beliefs are defended, the more deeply entrenched they become. As humans become emotionally intense about their beliefs, they become more difficult to overcome with logic or even outright facts that completely banish the belief, from a logical mind. Logic alone rarely can eliminate a belief. Typically, only other beliefs can help in unseeding beliefs.

But what about beliefs that aren't defended as much? What if the belief is not about being a Democrat or Catholic, Republican or Jew? What if the belief has much less involvement at the emotional level? How would you test this to know we weren't guessing about a philosophy of persuasion instead of a factual understanding? You would have to induce a belief, then try to change it.

Two groups of people were given brief descriptions and questionnaires about a quality that makes fire fighters successful or not at their job. (Anderson, Lepper, and Ross, 1980) One group was given substantial information that successful fire fighters are risk-taking individuals. The other group was given substantial information supporting the idea that fire fighters who are not successful tend to be risk-takers.

Then the experimenter totally discredited the information he gave the participants. "It was completely fictitious. I made it up. There is no evidence one way or the other." What happened?

Those who were told that good fire fighters are risk-takers continued to believe what they had come to believe.

Those who were told that good fire fighters are not risk-takers continued to believe what they had come to believe. There was no change.

In a later follow-up study, when the participants were asked *why* they believed what they had come to believe, their beliefs *strengthened* after they had given the causal (why) explanation.

Interesting note: Participants did not explain that the reason for their belief was because of the experiment they took part in. In each case it was attributed to other reasons. Many did not remember they even received this information in an experiment.

Now, here is some scary news about people's beliefs from research:

Two groups of people were surveyed for their beliefs (pro/con) about capital punishment as a deterrent to the crime of murder. Then each person in the two groups was given an article. Half the people in each group got an article that revealed that, in general, murder rates drop in states where capital punishment is made law. The other half of the people in each group were given an article that revealed that, in general, murder rates do not drop in states where capital punishment becomes law.

Results? The original beliefs were substantially changed—not in the direction of the evidence they were presented, but the opposite. Those who were shown that capital punishment didn't deter murder believed more strongly that it did if they had believed that in the first place.

In the next few chapters I'll show you what you need to know about the different types of beliefs, how they come to be so intensely defended, and the very few strategies that actually work in unplugging erroneous beliefs.

Many people attempt to persuade others by telling them what happened to themselves in a certain circumstance. ("I tried it and it really works!") or to someone like the client ("They are just like you and they tried it and it worked!") These strategies have been proven not to work.

What does work is when you can get clients to imagine *themselves performing the target behavior you need them to and experiencing (internally or externally) that behavior in some way.*

Covert Power with Skeptical and Gullible People

What do you think? Is resistance a thing that can be used up and replenished, like water in a tank?

Experiment

Students were divided into "gullible" and "skeptical" groups based upon interview questions. They were then further divided groups into four subgroups.

The first group was shown seven video clips of unfamiliar candidates running for office and where they stood on the issues. One group was asked to pay particular attention to the first clip. The other three groups were told to pay attention to the last. Two of these last three groups were shown a travelogue of Fiji before the last video was shown. One of these two remaining groups was told to think positively about Fiji. The other remaining group was told to make a list of all things that could go wrong on a trip to the islands. Finally, all subjects had to criticize each advertisement and candidate.

Gullible subjects used their resistance to advertising early on. They became less critical of the candidates as the experiment proceeded. The clips were shown in different orders to different students.

Reaction to the final clip depended on the approach that had been taken on the travelogue. If the subjects criticized the Fiji trip, they were more likely to look at the candidate positively. If they were more likely to look positively at the Fiji trip, they were more likely to criticize the candidate.

Skeptical subjects reacted differently. Skeptics were least critical of the first candidate and became increasingly more critical as time went on, regardless of the Fiji travelogue.

COVERT PERSUASION FACT

In gullible people, it is possible to *USE UP* resources for resistance, therefore making people less likely to resist your message.

Covert Power Project

How can you use up resistance early on with your clients and customers, making them more susceptible to your message?

3

Covert Strategies for Changing Beliefs

I n the previous chapter, we talked about how beliefs stick like glue and you learned some strategies to move people from "No" to "Yes!" In this chapter, we'll talk more about effective strategies for changing those sticky beliefs.

Option Attachment

Three bad things can happen after the sale:

One you already know: *Buyer's Remorse.*

One I showed you: *Anticipated Regret.*

The one I kept secret: *Option Attachment.*

I'm going to show you how (and why) these things will dramatically reduce your income if you continue as you have. I'm going to show you how to eliminate all three of these experiences so you can keep making sale after sale and more important, retain customers . . . forever.

There she is. She has a choice between two good options. (And that is what choice attachment is all about as you think about your life and selling situations.)

Guy #1 is attractive. Quiet. Not that sharp. Not an idiot. Goes hunting and fishing whenever he can. Plays pool out of season. Knows a lot of people especially from the bar and hunting. Average income. Survives the job.

She thinks that means that if she picks him, she'll have time for herself, time with her girlfriends, and probably an occasional party at the house with all of his friends over. Not a bad deal. And the freedom will be kind of nice. The lack of income will be a drawback but so what. It's not like he hates his job.

Guy #2 is also attractive. Sharp as a tack. Doesn't go play with boys. He has a few close friends that come over to the house but not many others. Likes to be at home more. Has a high income. Likes his work.

She thinks that means that he'll be home with her a lot. Lots of time together. Lots of time to get to know each other. Lots of time for playing, talking, cuddling. It would be nice not to have to worry about money. To be able to have no major stress there is very good, and he actually likes his work.

What does she do? And what happens to her *feelings* about her decision and the good guy she leaves behind?

She ponders the dilemma every day for weeks. Months. No matter who she chooses, one thing is certain (and she is oblivious to this fact): As soon as she chooses, the other guy will appear to be a much better choice than he appeared just days ago!

You'd think that she'd feel *good* about her decision. Relieved. Happy. Comfortable. But no, the opposite is the case.

This is what happens with your customers when they think about your product or service. You've never been shown this information by anyone anywhere in the world of psychology, marketing, or sales. So I will show you, and of course I'll show you how to overcome this challenging scenario.

This scenario is all about "option attachment."

Ponder this sentence: Your customer who thinks too long will feel that *choosing is losing*! Not a good thing.

This post-choice option attachment is not the same as buyer's remorse or anticipated regret. Buyer's remorse is regret at having purchased at all. Anticipated regret is the situation in which the customer experiences a feeling of wanting to avoid regretting his decision later.

No matter what the outcome of the choice the woman makes (even if her guy is nice, treats her well, she likes him and vice versa, it's all good), the other guy looks better than he did immediately before making the choice.

This is true in buying cars, investments, and just about everything else in life. And you can imagine the trouble that can come.

The woman has for months thought and thought about her decision. And this is indeed one of the core elements of the problem. The more someone has possessed something in her mind (imagination) or in real life (an actual external physical experience) the more she will feel disappointed when she realizes she has let that other option go.

In other words: Our woman is now seeing the guy she dumped as far more attractive than she ever thought and her emotional response is proving to her that she may have made a mistake.

And just what is this feeling she feels? Loss. She feels loss. Think of the feeling you get when someone you love dies or a pet dies. It's in that category.

Research studies show that it doesn't make much difference as to whether our woman friend has imagined these two relationships in detail or experienced them both. When she chooses her guy, the other guy becomes more valuable in her mind.

It makes no difference whether any of this is logical or not. Obviously she isn't going to end up with both guys. And remember, the guy she chose turns out to be a very good choice! Doesn't matter. The other guy still looks much better than he ever did because she owned him in her mind and maybe proximity for months. Now she has lost him because of her decision. Her feelings today reveal that her other guy option was better than she had thought. And it's proven by her feelings.

The other factor in the disappointment and feeling of loss? The degree to which she was attached to the other guy in her mind in the deliberation stage of her decision.

The scenario above is one that makes it easy to understand the concept of option attachment and sheds great light on some facts that you must know to retain customers and make decisions easier for your prospective customers.

1. Do not allow time for your customer to develop a sense of attachment or ownership in the deliberation stage. The deliberation should be fast. The sense of loss will happen if you don't.

2. If you must explore more than one option with your client, then rapidly move the client from the option that is the poorer choice to the option that is the better choice. Do not let the person begin to feel a sense of connection with an option that he will not ultimately get. Discuss an option, then make it obvious why it needs to be dismissed and dismiss it.

Of course there is much more about option attachment that costs you thousands of dollars per year in business . . . and yes, in the coming chapters I'll have much more to share with you about option attachment and how to deal with situations like this.

Covert Persuasion Power: What Convinces?

They have said no . . . or are right about there! You have a hotly debated subject and it's crucial to gain compliance. Perhaps your clients are being very resistant. You know they should agree because the answer is obvious, but they don't. You've tried everything (you think). Now what?

Here are some powerful ways that you can persuade the unpersuadable, and a few that they taught you to do and failed and you thought it was your fault. It wasn't.

The first powerful technique is "experiential influence." If you really want to be persuasive you have your greatest opportunity when your client experiences what you are selling. This was once known as the Puppy Dog Close. Take the puppy home, and how could anyone possibly return it?

This is why the guy that wanted to sell me a new driveway asked me to help him measure the driveway with his tape measure. (Like he doesn't know the size of my driveway.) It's why the real estate agent takes you through a house and then has you describe aspects of how you would be living there. It's why the automobile salesperson gives you the keys and lets you hit the road. It's why you can use Nero software for 10 days to burn your CDs and then pay.

Imaging Behavioral Scripts

A behavioral script is a precise set of instructions and images that you (typically verbally) give to your client, such as "Imagine walking into that IRS audit with someone there who will take all the heat for you and answer all the questions so you don't get pressured. You stay calm. I take the heat. That's the way it works and we keep your tax bill in check."

Specific Instructions and Images

a.   Imagining oneself performing a behavior changes the person's intentions toward the behavior.

If people can visualize themselves going to church, hearing the sermon, singing the songs, praying. and so forth, then they are more likely to change their mind and move in the direction of the imagined experience, in real life.

b. The more often someone imagines a behavioral script, the more his intention and attitude change toward the desired behavior.

   If you can get your client to think of whatever experience you want to have over and over again, or regularly over a period of days or weeks, he will become more comfortable with the experience and his attitude will change toward the behavior.

c. These changes do not occur when the main character in the imaging is not the person himself.

   Patterns that reference others, such as "I remember working with someone just like you and they did x, changed to y, and z happened" are not as effective. In selling this was called "Feel, Felt, Found." There is little benefit to this pattern when compared with other strategies of communication.

d. The intentions and attitudes hold at least three days when pondering the real life experience.

   Unlike high pressure selling tactics, these tools persist and stick for a few days.

This dispels some beliefs about visualization and reinforces others. More importantly, you now know what works. (I wish I had known this 20 years ago.)

There are two ways people attempt to persuade. One works. One doesn't.

Only highly evolved people will ever call into account their beliefs about anything. Beliefs about "how life is" or "how the world is" or "how you are" are all developed (and usually with little or no evidence beyond a single observation or repetition of being told something is so) fairly quickly. To actually think about a belief (or an opinion, an attitude) takes mental work and therefore people don't want to do it.

Persuading an intellectually lazy person to take up mental action is like getting a couch potato to run laps. Persuading an intellectual genius can be just as hard because they have spent so much time defending their beliefs on every level.

Changing beliefs can be tough. There are a couple of basic methods by which you can try to persuade someone else.

If you will recall, I shared with you that when people who hold a belief are presented with rock solid information showing their belief is false (remember the capital punishment as a deterrent to crime discussion in persuasion research) they simply internally defend their beliefs against the incoming new information and dig in deeper.

And remember, you've discovered that people's beliefs and opinions are sticky even when they are told by the originator of their belief that the originator completely lied to the person. Doesn't matter. The person still believes.

And, I've shared with you how people who have limited knowledge about something (like I do about cars, lawnmowers, and feminine hygiene products, for example) are not convinced by information of high quality (say statistical analysis) but by lots of different *points*.

Yes, people continue to play the Power Ball even though the odds of winning that big jackpot are roughly the same as dying seven times in plane crashes even in the post 9/11 world. You can't convince the average person otherwise because statistics mean nothing; their experience of seeing 10 people on TV who have won is all it takes to prove that they too have a chance. (They don't.)

OK, you'll need to keep those three factors in mind as we look at just what does change minds in addition to the very specific visual images I shared with you last time.

When people believe something, they believe it because of some reason(s).

- I saw the $100,000,000 lottery winner on TV. (It can happen to me!)

- Maybe they saw the UFO. (Wow, they must be real!)

- Maybe psychic "was right on the nose." (I knew it! They can see my past and future!)

- The economy soared under Clinton. (He was a great president.)

- The 9/11 tragedy happened during Bush's presidency. (He blew it. Lousy president.)

That's one way thoughts or experiences become beliefs. Someone sees it, they believe it. Then they generalize it to mean "always" and "forever."

"Can't trust those salespeople."

"Can't trust those politicians."

"Can't trust Catholic priests."

"Can't trust . . ."

". . . and YOU are an X therefore I don't trust you."

How are you going to change that?

People see something once and poof, it's true in every case for everyone. (It should be becoming obvious that prejudice is, unfortunately, normal to all of us in many areas and aspects of culture because of how beliefs are formed.) How are you going to change that? Beliefs, attitudes, prejudices, ideas . . . what's it going to take whether it's about you, your company, your business, anything?

If you can't get a person to accede to the imagination techniques I showed you in *Science of Influence*, then you are going to have to go to the next level.

Causal and Noncausal Arguments

An argument isn't a fight. An argument is a bunch of ideas/facts clustered together in such a way that they support a point of view. Could be logical or illogical, right or wrong, accurate or inaccurate. It is an argument. Creationism is an argument. Evolution is an argument. They are clusters of ideas/facts that are put together in such a way that they support a viewpoint.

Cause is about what makes something happen. It's one of two kinds of arguments that can make all the difference in the world in whether or not you hear "yes" or "no."

"You are a jerk because you used physical violence."

"You are a genius because you aced the exam."

"You are a psychic because you said his mother's name was Mary."

"You are a healer because you touched that person and he got well."

Those are causal statements. Something causes something else.

Then there are noncausal arguments. These are arguments that don't have anything to do with cause.

"Your life is in safe hands when flying. Only 1 in 2,000,000 will die on an airplane this year."

"Three times as many women die from heart disease as from breast cancer."

"People on the East Coast change their residence (on average) every 10 years."

"People on the West coast change their residence (on average) every five years."

"Children killed in school shootings are at all-time lows."

Those are *noncausal arguments.* They evaluate what has happened. They often use statistics to support the argument.

The argument, "I believe in God because I feel him in me," is a causal argument. "Look at all of the rest of the planets in the solar system. There is no life on any of them. There is here. That is a sign that God is working here and is real and present." A noncausal argument.

If you want to change a belief in ways other than action and imagination you will need to know which kind of argument is likely to work.

Beliefs can begin to change when something *outside* of the person triggers new or different representations on the *inside* of the person.

KEY: You must get the person to call into question his beliefs and not push a new belief structure onto him. Statistical evidence is almost useless in changing beliefs.

People continue to behave and believe in the face of overwhelming evidence to the contrary of their belief, when the evidence is *noncausal*. Statistics, evaluation, and noncausal arguments simply don't cut it in the belief change department. The proof is in the pudding.

Study about Causal/Noncausal Arguments

AIDS transmission was the subject of some argument and disagreement as recently as a few years ago. People held pretty strong beliefs about how people acquired AIDS and how they didn't.

One hundred sixty-seven adult participants agreed to participate in a study which would evaluate people's beliefs about AIDS and discover what kind of arguments would change those beliefs. The participants were divided into four groups. In one group, each person was given a booklet that detailed specifically how AIDS was not transmitted by casual contact. In the second group, each person was given a booklet that detailed statistically that AIDS is not transmitted by casual contact. In the third group, each person was given a booklet that combined both of the above approaches. In the fourth group, each person was given a self-assessment test that had nothing to do with AIDS.

Results?

The most effective way to change beliefs was with causal arguments. The second most effective way to change beliefs was the combined method. Least effective (not effective) were noncausal arguments. They didn't work.

Slusher and Anderson (1996) completed another more elaborate research project with more people and the extra variable that people could commit to take action on their new beliefs through volunteer work. Once again, those who read the causal arguments were changed the most. Those who committed to take action on their beliefs had even greater long-term change.

Great Thought Experiment

One night last year, Jay Leno (*The Tonight Show*) had George Carlin, Courtney Love, Ozzy Osborne, Ben Affleck, Kid Rock, Snoop Dog, Sylvester Stallone, and a host of other celebrities share their memories of their experiences on the decade-long hit TV show, *Friends*. It was absolutely hilarious. Great fun. I laughed and laughed.

Of course none of them was ever on the show. But a decade from now hundreds of thousands of people who watched the Tonight Show Thursday night, will remember one or more of those celebrities' guest spots on the show *Friends* with crisp and certain clarity. But, as I just said, none of them was ever on the show.

They will go through their *Friends* DVD collections and try to prove to their buddies that Ben Affleck really was on the show as a guest star in one episode. They'll remember what happened, whom he interacted with, and how funny it was. They'll know which show it was on. Of course, they'll never find it and be dumbfounded. They will tell their own friends that they were *positive* that they saw Ben on that one show.

OK, so people have weird memories . . . so what? What's it have to do with influence? Change? Selling? Marketing? Oh, just everything.

You see, if you can apply the gold you learn here, you will add clients, be far more influential, and save sales you would have lost every time in the past.

Applications

Wouldn't it be nice if you could facilitate your client's remembering how good you really are/were?

Wouldn't it be nice if you could keep a powerfully positive image and message about you and your product at the forefront of your client's mind all the time?

Wouldn't it be great if your client defended you and your services instead of calling them into question when talking with others?

How about virtually guaranteeing positive word of mouth marketing?

You've never read about this anywhere. You've never learned this from anyone. It's new and it's for you. Be prepared to be blown away.

People don't just remember it (an event, personal history, what happened an hour ago, how well your service worked for them last time, they often remember it in many different ways. Said another way, people have multiple memories and playbacks of actual events.

Quite often, people forgot their actual experience and instead remember incorrectly what their friend said about how the event happened. (Remember last year in *The Science of Influence* series, when I shared with you how by suggestion I could get you to remember an event that didn't happen?)

Sometimes they tell you that they did "it" and sometimes they tell you that they didn't. They might believe each story equally and completely forget their first recollection (thinking you have lost your mind!). Sometimes you were the good guy and sometimes you were the bad guy.

In the past, I've shared with you how the memory does not work. It doesn't record like a video camera. It collects information and shakes it up with other beliefs and attitudes and memories and external (environmental) influences and then gives you some output, and then the memory changes every time you bring it to mind.

If I have made your heart race about the absolute fragility of each person's opinion about you, your product, and service, I'll come back later and instill another roller coaster like feeling with what happens if you do not take this to heart and follow the strategies here.

Now let's go look at some background. You're on a jury. You hear an argument from an attorney or testimony from a witness. After listening to it, the judge tells you to ignore it and notes that the testimony is "stricken from the record."

Forget it? Impossible. *It's often made more powerful by the very suggestion of forgetting it!* (I'll show you how this happens later.)

What's interesting is that when you tell people that what they have just heard or seen is not true, whether from the source or someone else, the memory in no way deletes the information. In fact, when the correct information is finally given, shared, or shown to the individual, the person still is largely influenced by his original exposure to the information or experience.

Problem: Once a person has formed a belief, it is difficult to replace it or delete it.

Here's how people remember:

Participants in a research project were asked to figure out which suicide notes they were shown were real and which were fake. After they finished reporting which notes they thought were real and why, then those that they felt were fakes and why, they were given feedback about how accurate their guesses were.

Later, when they were asked how well they thought they would do when first presented with the task, the participants reported something fascinating. Participants who were told they did poorly remembered that when faced with the project, they thought they would do poorly. Those participants who were told they did well remembered that when faced with the project, they thought they would do well.

Participants were given feedback at random. Their reports were anything but. People remember thinking/predicting/guessing/estimating, what actually happened as opposed to what they thought would happen. This kind of research has been done over and over again, in different contexts, and the results come up the same every time.

As long as the person doesn't publicly communicate his thoughts/feelings before an event takes place, you can be certain he will remember predicting the result as it actually happened and not what they thought at the time.

In 1981 an article was shown to participants. It was a retrospective view of President Richard Nixon entitled, "Was Nixon a Crook?" The article completely discredited the notion that Nixon was a crook. The participants concluded that Nixon was indeed a crook. The suggestion of the article title was everything.

Wegner and Erber (1992, 1995) showed in different studies that telling someone not to think of something makes it more likely that the person will indeed think of it.

Indeed, this is how people think. In marketing, selling, therapy, and relationships your job is to head it off at the pass, if you can!

Otherwise, the person will have a belief that becomes a filter for all future communication about that subject. Attempting to change the filter is like getting me to change the oil filter on a car, an arduous task at best.

Lord, Ross, and Lepper (1979) call this "confirmation seeking." People will look to find what confirms their beliefs. It's that simple. These authors also found that people who believe X will not look for evidence to disconfirm their belief and when they do "see it" they will discount it.

When psychologists are given information that creates a belief (a kind of study that is far better controlled now than it has been in the past because of the huge long term effects of creating false beliefs in people), then told the information was made up, the psychologists still tend to believe what they were told or not discredit it completely when evaluating information. And these are people who should know how the mind works.

Think about These Amazing Facts of Human Behavior

70 percent of Americans once gave an opinion in a nationwide opinion poll about an act that didn't exist. Some felt the states should take care of the responsibility, some felt the government should. (People have an opinion on things that don't even exist!)

40+ percent of Americans chose the last option of three when asked what their opinion was on how easy getting a divorce should be in the USA. This was true regardless of which option was offered last. (People pick the last choice . . . remember this!)

Sales of jams in a store increased by 10 times when people could sample up to six jams vs. those days when the store offered 20 options. (More choices increase sampling . . . not sales!)

College students report cheating to be wrong in what appear to be anonymous forms. Given the opportunity, even those students reporting strong attitudes against cheating on exams immediately cheat when given the opportunity. (What people say and what they do are two very different things!)

When pollsters ask people what is the most important issue facing the nation people respond with hundreds of different answers that are completely different and in greatly differing percentages when pollsters ask people to choose from a list of options which is the most important issue facing the nation. (People don't tell you what they think; they select options from those *you give them!*)

When people are asked about such hot topics as nuclear weapons they will respond with opposite opinions depending on how the question is phrased. (Framing is the ball game!)

From these and dozens of other valid and reliable studies we conclude that:

1. People's opinions, thoughts, and desires are often molded by the questions they are asked.

2. People's thoughts, opinions, and desires are often created in the moment and have little or no relationship with what they will actually do or what they will believe later.

3. Many people have beliefs about things that are not real, based upon questions about things like nonexistent Acts of Congress and not knowledge.

Key 1: Most people are fairly automatic in their behavior. They see a commercial and because they believe what they see without critical thought, decide what drink to drink, restaurant to eat at, or tax preparer to use, all based upon suggestion.

Key 2: Once most people choose something, write something down, say something, whether it makes any sense or not, whether it is in their best interest or not, they tend to stick with that decision, regardless of how that decision was made.

Key 3: People don't like cognitive dissonance. Most can't hold two opposing thoughts in their minds so they simply pick the thought/decision/belief they currently hold and eliminate the rest without further consideration. This is called the law of consistency.

The Law of Consistency states that, "When an individual announces in writing (or verbally to a lesser degree) that he is taking a position on any issue or point of view, he will strongly tend to defend that belief regardless of its accuracy even in the face of overwhelming evidence to the contrary."

Your clients' past decisions and public proclamations dramatically influence their beliefs and attitudes. Once a person has publicly said, "I'll never X," they normally never do. Many people make public statements that they have not thought out, that often turn into beliefs and permanent attitudes. The reason is simple. We are taught that our word is our bond. When we say something you can count on us.

Super Key! Who Sticks with their Decisions?

A recent research study had subjects make decisions among various choices:

Group A was asked to "remember their decision."

Group B was asked to "write their decisions on a magic slate and then pull the sheet up, erasing their decision."

Group C was asked to write down their decisions on paper with ink and hand them in to the researchers.

Which group stuck with their decisions? Right. Group C stuck with their decisions more than 75 percent of the time. Group B kept their decisions half the time, and Group A tended to change their minds. The lesson is to get your client to write things down as he participates in the sales process. He could write down anything from goals for the coming year to what he would really like in a car, a house, a stock portfolio, or a vacation time share package. The key is to get a pen in the client's hand and have him write!

Never ask for a question which will pin the client down to a permanent "no" response.

4

Covert Persuasion 101: The Tactics

There are dozens of ways to communicate with clients and prospects. The *Covert Persuasion Tactics* in this chapter are an exclusive collection of the closely guarded and little known subtle tactics used by the most successful professional persuaders.

When we are making our presentations and proposals to others in the business world, we should note that the following tactics are valuable in a one-on-one lunch date, afternoon committee meeting, or a seminar or speech before a group of 1,000. These tactics have been proven effective. While not every tactic works in every situation, you now have in your hands a very special catalog of techniques to choose from to get the result you want in almost any situation and with almost anyone.

There are 55 tactics described in the following pages. You might want to read through all 55 so that you are aware of all of these techniques before returning to them and finding out all the ways you can use them in your encounters.

Becoming aware of these tactics will not only make you a sharper, more successful communicator, but will also equip you with the information you need to become a better, wiser, and more intelligent consumer. Let's get started.

	Rapidly Build Resonant Rapport

COVERT PERSUASION TACTIC #1

Rapport can be defined as being "in sync" with another person. Generally, people are more likely to have good rapport with someone else if they like that person. How do you know if you have rapport with someone? Ask yourself this question: *Does the person respond to me in a genuinely positive manner?*

If so, you have some degree of rapport. I was at a seminar once and heard Zig Ziglar say, "They don't care how much you know, until they know how much you care." You want to begin to develop a sense of empathy and sincere curiosity about others. Rapport occurs on different levels of communication. You can be technically skilled at acting and appear to have rapport, but if you don't sincerely care about your client and the people you are working with, what is the point?

People are very good at sensing if you are sincere. Something in their gut (or their intuition) will tell them to trust you or to turn you off. And, like most first impressions, it will happen in an instant, even before they're consciously aware.

You probably already know that you can facilitate rapport by matching and mirroring another person's body position. (Sitting in a similar position, moving as he moves as in dancing.)

Another way to establish rapport is to talk about common territory subjects. You both like the Red Sox? You both fish or play golf? If you know that, utilize that knowledge. That's worth talking about. Content matters in rapport too.

With a little practice, rapport skills will flow so naturally that you will also be unaware (consciously) of exactly what is going on—all you'll know is that it's working.

The next couple of Covert Persuasion techniques deal exclusively with rapport. If you do not have rapport, it's more difficult to persuade others. Without rapport there is no trust, no belief, and often no persuasion.

Rapport *(n.)* a relationship, especially one of mutual trust or emotional affinity.

	Use Content to Build Rapport
COVERT PERSUASION TACTIC #2	Discover what your target's interests are, and if you're not in tune with their interests, learn about them. People like to talk about what they

are interested in. It lowers mental defenses and allows in new information—your new information.

You can build a great deal of rapport, and even long term friendships, by showing and experiencing interest in what is important to other people. Sincerely sharing the experiences of your client's hobbies, lifestyle, and interests is called "using content to build rapport." Put simply, you are finding out what's of interest to the other person and using it to strengthen the bond between the two of you.

Dale Carnegie, Zig Ziglar, and many others talk about developing and demonstrating a sincere interest in the other person. Why? Because, if genuine, it allows a connection to happen on an emotional level that will allow you to have power and influence with the person that you otherwise would never have.

When you use content to build rapport, you are using something naturally of high interest to the other person. Fundamentally, we are all selfish. Think about yourself for a moment. When you are shown a group picture that you are a part of, whom do you look at first in that picture? Of course, you look at yourself. And while we're on the topic of you, when talking with others in almost any setting, you're most comfortable talking about the things *you* like, right?

This is exactly why using content (that other people find interesting or connect with emotionally) is such a powerful tool. When used properly, they will feel strongly that you are very much like they are and that it's okay to trust and like you. From this point on, your persuasion attempt will fall on receptive ears.

But it's not always easy. What if there are no visual cues like personal things in the target's environment? Then you'll have to use "processes" to build rapport, and that's the next covert persuasion technique.

Use Processes to Build Rapport

COVERT PERSUASION TACTIC #3

There is more to building rapport than swapping fishing stories. Becoming in-sync with another person or group can take a great deal of skill, in addition to the sincere interest that is necessary in building relationships.

Many people will not feel comfortable discussing their families, hobbies, and lifestyle with you if they've just met you. How does the ice get broken when stories are very uncomfortable for your target? Many of the people you will want to persuade were taught as children not to talk to strangers. They were taught to keep private matters private. How do you help these people become comfortable with you?

First, *doing* the same activity or processes they are involved in will help you to appear more similar to them. There will be a common or very similar experience that can help bond the two of you (or you to your audience). This common experience will help your target feel comfortable with you and everything you say.

What types of "processes" are available for you to build on?

- Type of work.

- Place or setting for work.

- Business or corporate structure.

- Family or social structure/status.

As you can see, there are many levels and situations where you can use the similar processes that you both are involved in as a point of connection. You can demonstrate through act or shared experience that you are "just like them," so it's safe to trust you and safe to follow or accept your suggestion to comply with your request.

Connecting with people is critical to your long-term success.

"We must all hang together, or assuredly we shall all hang separately."

—Benjamin Franklin

COVERT PERSUASION TACTIC #4

Synchronize with Your Target

When in doubt, an effective way to begin building rapport with anyone is by "pacing." Synchronization is essentially synonymous with the terms "matching" and "mirroring." Simply stated, be like your client. We all like people who we believe are like us.

Your client will like you more, or have rapport with you more quickly, if he/she gets the feeling that you are just like him/her. One way to do this is with "pacing." There is a fine line here that you do not want to cross. You do not want it to ever appear that you are copying or mimicking the other person. If the other person believes you are trying to manipulate him, then your persuasion attempt just went from covert to overt, and because of that you will fail. Instead, you must be subtle. Synchronization is the key.

There are two levels of using this technique successfully. First, you must begin where the other person is; he must feel that you are just like him. He must identify with you on some level for you to have any power to persuade. Once you have connected on some level with the other person, you can then begin to set the pace and he will follow. We're talking about leading. There is more information to follow in this area so that all your efforts remain covert.

"The truth isn't the truth until people believe you, and they can't believe you if they don't know what you're saying, and they can't know what you're saying if they don't listen to you, and they won't listen to you if you're not interesting, and you won't be interesting until you say things imaginatively, originally, freshly."

—William Bernbach

COVERT PERSUASION TACTIC #5

Synchronize Voices

Imagine the person you are communicating with is in an upset mood. He has a sharp edge to his voice. Many people try to cheer this person up with a smile and cheery story. This doesn't work. *When in doubt, pace your target.*

If your target has an edge in his voice, let your voice have an edge, even if just briefly. This vocal pacing will help put you in-sync with your client. Eventually you will *lead* your client out of this negative state (if that is necessary) and into a different or more receptive state of mind.

There's more you can do than simply match the tone of your clients. Since we all speak with a measurable average number of words per minute, you can match their rate of speech. These two things alone will be powerful and subtle.

As with most steps in covert persuasion there are some things you do not want to do. When using your voice, don't copy the verbal ticks of your target. From stuttering to saying "ummm" all the time or constant throat clearing, these are things to avoid during pacing. If you do these things, obviously your tactics will become overt and then it's over.

COVERT REMINDER

Building rapport is fundamental to Covert Persuasion. One specific strategy is to speak with the same rate and tone as your target.

COVERT PERSUASION TACTIC #6

Synchronize Breathing

Breathing is one of the most unconscious activities. This Covert Technique, if done correctly, will literally put you in the same rhythm as your client.

Your client will sense that rhythm and feel more comfortable with you. Our research shows that simply by pacing another person's breathing, inhaling when they do, exhaling when they do, increases the rapport between two people. That result holds true even if this is the only Covert Persuasion technique you use; it's that powerful.

Sometimes, you'll actually begin to think the same type of thoughts and feel some of the same kinds of feelings when you match breathing rate and depth. People who run together for exercise will end up breathing in similar patterns. They become very in-tune with each other.

Most people don't think about pacing breathing as a rapport-building tool. It's usually so far below the conscious radar when we interact with another person that we often forget it ourselves. But if we look back in detail on a successful "persuasion attempt" it often is found to be a key element.

COVERT PERSUASION TACTIC #7	**Synchronize Posture and Movement but Beware**

Unlike pacing someone's breathing, pacing someone's posture is much simpler, but be careful. If you assume the exact same body position and posture as your target he may feel uncomfortable.

You want your client to feel so comfortable that his defenses go down and your request for compliance is heard with very little involvement or critical thinking. Again, you don't want to make your clients feel like you are mimicking them.

Nodding or Shaking Your Head May Even Influence Your Own Thoughts

Doesn't it blow your mind that you often have no idea why you feel so strongly about some things (good or bad) and you don't even know why? Everything from the environment to your beliefs to your unconscious conditioning changes your thoughts. I want you to see the unexpected way that your physical movements change your thoughts. Read carefully; it's not what you are expecting.

Nodding your head doesn't mean you'll agree with whatever you are hearing. One of the most surprising things we found is that if you're thinking negative thoughts while you're nodding, this actually strengthens your disapproval.

When you nod your head to signal approval or shake your head to show disapproval, it's not just sending a message to others, you may also be influencing yourself.

A new study (Petty and Brinol, 2003) showed that these simple movements influenced people's agreement with an editorial they heard while nodding or shaking their head. Researchers found that other body movements such as writing with a non-dominant hand can also influence attitudes, even about important issues such as self-esteem.

The study found that nodding your head up and down is, in effect, telling yourself that you have confidence in your own thoughts, whether those thoughts are positive or negative. Shaking your head does the opposite: It gives people less confidence in their own thoughts.

In another study, the researchers told 82 college students that they were testing the sound quality of stereo headphones, particularly how the headphones would perform when they are being jostled, as during dancing or jogging.

Half the participants were told to move their heads up and down (nodding) about once per second while wearing the headphones. The other half were told to move their heads from side to side (shaking) while listening on the headphones.

All of the participants listened to a tape of a purported campus radio program that included music and a station editorial advocating that students be required to carry personal identification cards.

After listening to the tape, the participants rated the headphones and gave their opinions about the music and the editorial that they heard. The study found that head movements did affect whether they agreed with the editorial. But the effect is more complicated than might be expected.

The study found that nodding your head up and down is, in effect, telling yourself that you have confidence in your own thoughts whether those thoughts are positive or negative. Shaking your head does the opposite: It gives people less confidence in their own thoughts.

Participants in this study who heard an editorial that made good arguments agreed more with the message when they were nodding in a "yes" manner than shaking in a "no" manner. This is because the nodding movements increased confidence in the favorable thoughts people had about the good arguments compared to shaking.

However, students who heard an editorial that made poor arguments showed the reverse pattern. These students agreed less with the message when they were nodding than when shaking. This is because the nodding movements increased confidence in the negative thoughts they had about the poor arguments compared to shaking.

Another study found the same results occurred even when participants were evaluating something they knew very well: themselves. And it occurred with a completely different kind of body motion: handwriting.

In this case, the participants were asked to write down three good or bad qualities they thought they had with respect to their planned careers. But some were told to write with their right hand, while others were told to write with their left hand (all were determined to be right-handed). They were then asked to rate how confident they were in the thoughts they had listed.

Results showed that the participants had more confidence in their thoughts when they wrote them with their right (dominant) hand than when they wrote with the left (non-dominant) hand.

It is significant that these body movements can even affect confidence in thoughts about issues in our lives that are important to us and that we have thought about deeply, like our own self-evaluations.

COVERT PERSUASION TRICK

If your target is in a "stuck state" and your persuasion attempt is not moving in the direction you would like it to, move your body, stand up, walk around the room, walk to the restroom and back. It's a proven fact that emotion can come from motion. You'll change your target's state of mind if you are able to get your target to physically move. Changing physical position changes internal states.

COVERT
PERSUASION
TACTIC #8

Testing Synchronization

Developing a sincere interest in relationships and friendships with others is the first step in the persuasion process. Getting in-sync with your client is the second step. Leading comes third. This is where the magic happens. The first time you successfully lead someone, you'll be surprised by how easily it can be done.

You know leading is successful when the person follows you.

If he does follow your lead (a small physical move by you is mirrored by him), then you have him at the unconscious level. You're almost ready to begin your presentation, but first you have to confirm that you are truly in rapport. A couple of extra seconds in this stage can prove critical. You want to make sure you "have them" and then begin to alter your body language, your voice tone, rate, or pitch. You'll know the other person is following you when he makes a similar movement or alters his voice in a similar manner.

Practice working your target just up to the threshold of consciousness—and stop before he becomes consciously aware.

COVERT
PERSUASION
TACTIC #9

Alter the Tone, Rate, or Pitch of Your Voice

There are times when leading with your body or gestures is not going to be helpful. In these cases (and in some face-to-face communication) you lead by altering one of your vocal qualities. You may, for example, increase your speaking rate a little bit and induce a more enthusiastic attitude in the tone of your voice to help you bridge the conversation to your product. The context of your discussion will help determine when and if this is appropriate.

When you notice that the client follows your lead with a more enthusiastic voice, an increased rate of speech, and a higher or lower tone of voice, you can feel assured you have successfully developed rapport.

There was a very interesting social psychology experiment done on a college campus where many sets of male/female couples were paired up, and for 20 minutes they were allowed to say only three words to each other. However, these three words had to be said with all the love and passion they could muster. What were the three words? "Pass the salt." That's it. Sounds odd, doesn't it? Well, when those three words were said with direct eye contact and with all the love and passion that you would say "I love you" to your wife or husband, the results were amazing.

Out of the two dozen pairs of students that participated, several started dating immediately afterwards, and yes, believe it or not, a couple of marriages resulted!

Why? Well, it's been said that, "it's not what you say, but how you say it that matters." There is so much meaning carried in the tone, rate, pitch, and pace of your voice that the words are only a small part of what's really being said. Your voice is an entire force unto itself.

COVERT PERSUASION TACTIC #10

Induce Reciprocity

The entire process of building rapport is built on the foundation of concern, caring, compassion, interest, and a desire for the wellbeing of your client. Pacing and leading is a process that creates comfort for you and your target because you are moving along at a pace that is appropriate for your target.

The entire process does not necessarily take very long. It could be as quick as 20 seconds, or as long as an hour or more. After you've established rapport, the next step is to begin *your* presentation. There are many ways to begin, but one of the most effective is to give your target something. It has to be something of perceived value. Giving away junk does not induce reciprocity. Of course, you have to give this gift to your client with no expectation of a return. The resulting power of this principle will not disappoint you. If something of genuine perceived value is given to your target, he or she will feel compelled to return your generosity, usually with something of similar value. This return may come directly from the person you helped, or it may come from contacts of his in the future if the person you helped is not in a position to directly return the favor.

COVERT PERSUASION FACT

Initially people don't buy into ideas, product, services, candidates, or causes—-they buy *you!*

When we induce reciprocity, we must do so with the future expectation of absolutely nothing. However, more often than not, the favor does come back to us multiplied, but we may not realize the source.

$10,000 COVERT PERSUASION TACTIC

Give away something of perceived value to someone and they will feel compelled to do likewise.

COVERT PERSUASION TACTIC #11

Make the Damaging Admission

From the time of the earliest philosophers, it has been recognized that to win another person to your way of thinking, it is very helpful to admit a weakness in your case before the other person does. Admitting a fault or damaging admission actually allows you to be viewed as far more credible.

People are more skeptical today than at any time in history. They're always looking for the catch or the exception. When you admit a small flaw, drawback, or negative, then you're immediately viewed as more honest and as someone the other person would want to do business (or cooperate) with.

Lawyers know this covert persuasion technique and make excellent use of it. In fact, if you watch *Law & Order* or any of the legal dramas on TV, you'll often hear them talking about how there may be one or two facts that they don't want the other side to bring up because it may hurt their case. So, what do they do? That's right, *they bring it up* and put as favorable a spin on it as possible and then move right along. This way, when the other side does bring up the point, it's not as damaging.

$10,000 COVERT PERSUASION TRICK

Be eager to point out any negative aspects of your proposal. This accomplishes two important things. First it makes you appear far more trustworthy, and second, it allows your target to be set at ease since you are doing his job of finding drawbacks in the proposal.

COVERT PERSUASION TACTIC #12

Share Part of You with Them

Show your confidence in your client by helping him with one of his potential problems. In other words, offer to help him in any way that you can. Can you make a phone call for him as a referral? Can you help him bring more business to his store by taking 50 business cards? What can you do to freely help him with his business that is above and beyond the scope of your sales call? *Offer to help.*

I always go above and beyond to help people. I give massive

amounts of help because it's the right thing to do. There is always a return when I help. I will make a phone call, or personally respond to e-mail. I will literally share a part of me with them.

When you share in this manner, it helps others to realize you are just like them. Once this has happened, I know I have a customer for life, someone who will actively and positively mention my work to other people.

Looking a little deeper into the psychology of why this is a Covert Technique reveals that this is more than just rapport building, it is a personal connection. It is the type of connection that bonds people and makes them feel comfortable enough to drop all defenses.

COVERT PERSUASION TACTIC #13

Find and Point Out the Common Enemy

Nothing binds two people, groups, or nations like a common enemy. Find their enemy and align yourself with their viewpoint. Do they hate the IRS? Do the same people try to hurt your mutual businesses?

A common enemy may not be easy to find; however, if you figuratively back up and look at the bigger situation, you will easily find a common enemy that you can both join forces to fight together.

Do you remember how September 11th united this country like nothing else in recent history? There were U.S. flags flying everywhere, even on cars. We were a closely united country. Think back to that time shortly after the attack. The feeling of national pride in those you talked to was powerful. It was so powerful that you would feel differently when you would talk about it with others. You would feel differently when you saw those haunting pictures of the aftermath on TV.

I'll never forget a TV news piece that documented the day. There was such an overwhelming amount to convey—who, why, how, and so forth. But instead, the reporter simply put the silent video together with a very haunting but emotionally powerful piece of music and said nothing. It was the most powerful stream of visual and emotional material I have ever seen. The lack of a "talking head" or expert analyzing the day, total lack of anyone saying anything, stopped me in my tracks and made me look. You could hear the real noise of the day on the video, sirens, silence, and see the electronic rescue beacons from the fallen emergency workers. The memory of this particular video/audio package still gives me chills to this day.

The events of 9/11 were a common enemy of uncommon strength. Let's back off the intensity of that and talk about the types of real-world common enemies that you will be able to use when you covertly persuade others to your way of thinking.

First, there are the common internal enemies of all businesses like the rising cost of everything they buy, the rising cost of health care coverage for their employees, and the constant pressure to sell more and earn more every day to cover these ever rising expenses.

Second are the common external enemies like competition. You both may find a common enemy in a competitor. This may be a company or even another country.

Third, of course, there are personal enemies. You may be able to form an inner company alliance against a particular person so that he does not advance (as they do on the TV show, *Survivor*).

Regardless of where the enemy is, identify him, her, or it and align yourself with your target *against* this enemy. There is power in combining forces. Successfully accomplished, you are easily seen by your target as being on his side. Now anything you say is accepted more quickly and with less conscious analysis. This is exactly what we want to happen because, remember, Covert Persuasion is all about getting what you want and bypassing the critical analysis of the

other person so your idea, suggestion, or proposal is readily accepted
and acted upon.

	Tell a Short Story about Someone Like
COVERT	**Your Target**
PERSUASION	
TACTIC #14	If you can build a collection of stories about

people who have become your clients, followed
your business advice, or somehow benefited from interacting with
you, then you can utilize this Covert Persuasion tool.

Tell today's target about another person who recently complied
with your request. This other person should be someone he reminds
you of, someone he will also immediately feel is similar to his own
company or situation. Your target will instinctively assimilate himself
into your story and you'll have almost instant rapport.

Recently, I was given the opportunity to talk to two CEOs of
Fortune 1000 companies. My task was to get each one to speak at
two different events, each to be attended by about 300 high-level
business people. At the start, I did not know these two individuals;
however, when I told each one a very short story about how the
other one was considering accepting the invitation to speak, they
immediately felt more comfortable about discussing the possibility
further.

The turning point in those discussions was the very short
story I told each one about someone just like him who had been
given this same opportunity and was seriously considering our invitation.

People instinctively put themselves into the story you are
telling, that's why people laugh and cry when watching a really
good movie. They place themselves in the situation and identify
with the person in the story (who you've made sure is almost ex-

actly like them or facing almost exactly the same situation). This identification is easy.

You want it to be easy for your target to mentally picture himself in the story, and to do what the person in the story did (buy from you, agree with you, or accept your suggestion).

COVERT PERSUASION TACTIC #15	**Give Respect**

Sincerely show respect for your targets via a compliment. Always be looking for things to like or admire about other people. Compliment them openly. A little respect goes a long way. This is true because fundamentally we want the respect and admiration of the people we respect and admire. We also want to be respected and admired. That may sound like a lot of double-speak, but reread it carefully. Respect is such a strong force that it warrants your close attention . . . *your respect!*

"Without feelings of respect, what is there to distinguish men from beasts?"

—Confucius

$10,000 COVERT PERSUASION TRICK

When you exhibit genuine respect for your target, you will be received more openly and with a less critical eye on your intentions, primarily because you are giving the person one of the core things he craves: respect from others.

"To sit back and let fate play its hand out, and never influence it is not the way man was meant to operate."

—John Glenn, astronaut, U.S. senator

COVERT STRATEGY #1
The Wal-Mart Strategy

Do this:

Change the price of your product to end in a seven.

Numerous Internet marketers report greater sales with products that end in a "7".

Scientific research shows that the last number can make a big difference in sales. When the last number in a price (like $499) changes the first number in the price ($500), it makes the most difference.

Something that costs $550 is not going to be significantly helped by a $549 or $547, but a $600 price will be greatly helped by a $597 or $599.

COVERT PERSUASION TACTIC #16

Knock Their Socks Off

Blow them away with an astonishing claim, an amazing fact, or something that few would know.

Show them something amazing that no one else has shown them. Make the biggest claim you can substantiate.

People like to be positively surprised. Given a new fact or situation, it's easier to say "yes" to what you want because, in doing so, your target can save face.

Making a new decision (to follow you) is always easier when you help someone discover a new fact. This allows your targets to rest easy because they can be certain that their past decisions were right based on the information they had at the time. But now that they know this new piece of information, they can feel comfortable coming to a new decision.

Knocking their socks off is an expression of the unexpected. It is that extra piece of product or service or information that shocks them and maybe their view of the world. This opens their minds up to accept new ideas and generally puts them in a more receptive state of mind.

Unfortunately, it is all too common to have not even one sock knocked off.

Recently, I took my car into the dealership for an oil change and, believe it or not, walked out paying over $600 for repairs. Talk about *persuasion!* But my dad always told me never take chances on repairs when it comes to tires and brakes. And, of course, guess what these repairs were? Exactly.

It's disappointing to realize how many opportunities that dealership had to make my experience outstanding—and control every aspect—but instead, it was uneventful and disappointing, unfortunately normal.

So, do whatever it takes to add that little extra effort and knock their socks off, you'll be amazed at how receptive to new ideas they are when they're without socks!

$10,000 COVERT PERSUASION TRICK
Present the product they should buy, last. The target is compelled to own something and normally will take the last option.

COVERT PERSUASION TACTIC #17

Always Give More Than You Promised

Napoleon Hill, author of the classic book *Think and Grow Rich*, often used the phrase, "go the extra mile." It means to go out of your way or deliver more quickly or with higher quality for your customer than does your competitor.

Going the extra mile subtly persuades the other person to

continually seek you out because he knows he will not only get what's expected but can count on you to do the little extra that makes it special to do business with you instead of someone else. After comparison shopping, such people will choose you over other options.

One of the most important of all the techniques, it allows the customer to come out better than he expected by getting more than you promised.

Lou Holtz, a famous football coach, knew the power of this technique. During one halftime talk to his team, who were losing 42-0, Holtz showed a highlight reel of unbelievable second efforts to get the ball, stay in bounds, or score. He then told the players that each of them was on the team not because he could give it his all on every play; the coach told them every player on every team does that. It's expected. He then told them the reason they were on his team was because of their ability to make that critical second effort on each play. The second effort is the difference-maker. His team went out and won the game.

Use Understatement Power

COVERT PERSUASION TACTIC #18

After making your big fat claim, support it with the power of understatement. In other words, if your mutual fund portfolio has a track record of 12 percent return per year over the last 10 years, then understate that by saying "Now, if you average 10 percent per year . . ." For 10 years your fund has earned a 12 percent return, but you are being conservative for your client, and he knows it and appreciates it.

You are setting up a valuable expectation on the part of those you do business with. They will soon expect you to *overdeliver* on your assignments. You don't exaggerate. You understate, and that makes your claims and statements much easier to work with.

Be Precise: Then Beat Your Precision

COVERT PERSUASION TACTIC #19

If you know that a certain automobile is going to get your client 19 miles per gallon, tell him that. Then, tell him a secret: "But if you use a certain brand of oil, you can add an extra three miles per gallon of gas and that translates into hundreds of dollars saved each year."

Being specific adds credibility and believability to your entire argument. When you have the details and you know their impact, you are on solid ground and harder to attack. People don't like to hear round numbers. "You'll make a million dollars." "You'll have a 50 percent increase in sales." People unconsciously feel better when they have extremely specific information.

I have always kept a notebook by my phone at work. I can always tell you exactly the date, time, and content of every phone call I have had. While at first glance that seems like a strange habit, it has saved me more than once and, most important, it has proven to be a very strong persuasion tool.

There have been many times when someone will recall having a different conversation than what actually took place. Due to my precision, I can quickly look up the details. For example, I can easily say, "Are you sure about that, Bob, because I have notes from our last conversation dated October 14th at 3:10 P.M.; we talked about XYZ and we agreed that 4 percent was the solution . . . remember?"

Having that kind of precision has helped me so many times that I've lost count. The bottom line is, *be precise . . . then beat your precision!*

Get It Done Faster, Easier, Better

COVERT PERSUASION TACTIC #20

You live in an age when everyone you meet wants everything better, cheaper, faster, and easier. So promise what you can and then deliver, but add that little extra effort that makes all the difference.

Speed usually gets the sale (or the cooperation, agreement, etc). People take action faster when they can get something faster. Think about our fast-moving society. There's Federal Express to send your package fast, McDonald's to feed you fast, lottery tickets to make you rich fast, and shirts that get laundered in one hour. Even entire CDs now download in a matter of seconds.

Promising a fast, easy, and better result will often win the cooperation of your target. Why?

- Fast: because people want things *now!*
- Easy: because people are generally *lazy!*
- Better: because people feel they are entitled to "better!"

These three tricks have the greatest power when combined. For example: "You'll get it this afternoon instead of next week, plus I'll do all the work so you don't have to, and finally we'll all enjoy the result much better than the way it was, okay?"

COVERT STRATEGY #2

The McDonald's Strategy

Do this:

Add on a smaller purchase to the existing order by asking a question. McDonald's does it with, "Would you like fries with that?" The question added millions to the bottom line by slightly increasing the size of each sale. It's a much better question than "Will that be all?" That adds nothing.

Once a man has bought the suit, he will have no problem buying the comparatively inexpensive tie. Having bought the car, adding the stereo system is pennies on the dollar.

Find out what your "fries" are and build a question around them. You'll be adding dollars directly to the bottom line and increasing your customer's total satisfaction at the same time.

COVERT PERSUASION TACTIC #21

Be On the Edge of Your Seat

Pay attention, with bated breath, to every word your target has to say. It should be clear that what he has to say is the most important thing in either of your worlds at that moment. When you are genuinely excited, sincerely respectful, and very hard working, your target will seem to demand to help you accomplish your goals.

This really comes down to the power of one word: *listen!*! I have been to social functions where I've made it a point to simply ask questions and allow the other person to talk. People love to talk, and they really love to talk about themselves.

When you listen intensely, you gain favor with the other person, who after a short time will usually feel compelled to listen to you.

Sometimes I go into a meeting and all I do is intensely listen. That's it. At the end of the meeting, the other person often tells me what a "great conversationalist" I am. I really didn't say anything . . . on purpose! The next time I meet this person he will seek me out. Such people have rapport with you from this moment on, and every time you approach them with anything you are likely to get a "yes" response.

COVERT PERSUASION TACTIC #22

Ask for Compliance

This is literally just the start of the relationship. Your clients know that you have their best interest at heart. They know that you're going to be there for them when problems need to be solved. The simplest way to ask for compliance is to state the benefit your prospects will get by going ahead with your suggestion and adding, ". . . so, let's get started, okay?"

It's that simple. If all the groundwork of the previous steps has been done well, you're almost guaranteed to gain the voluntary compliance of the other person. But the key is to ask.

Many people will do all the necessary groundwork up to the request for compliance. They will work very hard perfecting the setting, and content, use Outcome Based Thinking, and in the end they never ask for the other person to do business with them.

There are many ways to ask others to go along with you, and one of the best is the "assumed okay." Simply say, "This looks like the best course of action, so, let's get started, okay?" It's that simple! But it's also easy not to do it. So remember, ask!

You miss 100 percent of the shots you don't take. Take a lot of shots.

COVERT PERSUASION TACTIC #23	### Induce the Sense of Scarcity

When we find out that something we want is limited in quantity, time, color, or options, our desire for it increases. To put it another way, if we can't get something easily, then our desire for it increases.

Using this to covertly persuade the other person is powerful and might sound something like this, "Now, because only 2,000 were made like this and each one is numbered, let's reserve yours right now. I'd hate to see you miss out on an opportunity like this."

$10,000 COVERT PERSUASION TRICK
Scarceness Awareness!
Your customer/target must be made aware that something about you, your services, or your product is scarce. Scarcity can include the quantity of the product, the time you have to spend with someone, or a number of specific products at a special low price.

The persuasion attempt will let prospects know that there is a very real possibility that they will not get their product because stock or time will run out. It's also your job to make clear to them exactly how and what they will lose.

COVERT PERSUASION TACTIC #24

Open the Door to a Friend

We like people who we think are just like us. We become quick friends. We trust and follow our friends. We all have a deep desire to be liked. This is why friends will often dress in very similar clothes, travel in the same social circles, and even drive similar cars. We want to be liked, so we think, act, and do what our friends are doing.

As salespeople we can use this to our advantage simply by supplying our prospects with a list of people (or companies) just like them—maybe even someone they actually know personally who has also bought your product or service and is now enjoying the benefits.

> *"If you would win a man to your cause, first convince him that you are his sincere friend."*
>
> —Abraham Lincoln

$10,000 COVERT PERSUASION TRICK
Allow your target to see you and/or your products or services linked to the respected, the famous, and the experienced and your probability of the "yes" response is heightened dramatically.

COVERT STRATEGY #3
Create a Frequent Buyer Program!
Do this:

Of the three ways to grow any business or increase any stream of income, this is the fastest and most powerful. Create a program of rewards for frequent purchases.

For example, when I use my Visa card, I earn points toward $5.00 certificates I can use at Borders Books to buy more and more books. Those certificates bring me back to the bookstore more often than I otherwise might go. There's also the "coffee club" at the local convenience store where my card gets punched, and once I've purchased six coffees, my seventh is free.

Your airline has a "miles"card; your American Express Card might double as a "Starwood Card" where you get points for every purchase, which builds toward free nights at any hotel in their network all over the world.

How can you give your customer more of an incentive to buy from you more often?

COVERT PERSUASION TACTIC #25

Associate the Known to the Unknown

There is real persuasion power in connecting a new idea that is not known or easily understood to something that is very familiar and trusted by your prospect. Sometimes it can be simply stated. For example, the following statement relates the new and unknown product to the old and familiar 660DX. *"It's just like your old 660DX, but now with the addition of a flux capacitor that uses 50 percent less power, saving you $5,200 per year!"*

Not only is association a linking tool from the known to the unknown, it is also a tool used to link something new or improved with *someone* we like, admire, or respect.

For example, do you remember when Michael Jordan did commercials for underwear? What does he know about underwear that you or I don't? That's right, nothing. Michael Jordan is simply someone that a lot of people like, admire, and respect. Companies will pay millions of dollars to get a famous celebrity to endorse their product hoping that the consumers (you) will want to be just like him—"just like Mike."

Association is also a powerful tool without any humans involved. What do you think of when you see a Clydesdale horse? Budweiser. Why? They've successfully associated their product with these magnificent horses.

Another powerful form of association is the endorsement or testimonial. Whether it's the words of a customer on their own letterhead that you show to a new prospect, or it's the spoken words of endorsement by a superior at work, having someone who is independent and credible say that you or your product is great is a key that unlocks the mind of your target. These testimonials and endorsements are read as unbiased, credible, independent, honest, and true. They are far more believable to your client than if you said the exact same thing. So, find those independent sources to vouch for you and your product. It is one very powerful Covert Persuasion technique.

When someone that you like, admire, and respect tells you there is someone you should get to know, deal with, buy from or hire, you are more likely to turn off the critical faculties of your mind and accept this suggestion based on trust.

Let Them Feel Part of the Group

COVERT PERSUASION TACTIC #26

There is power in the group. We like to belong. Even very rebellious teenagers will say they are their own persons and that they are an "original," but take a close look at their friends.

They wear the same clothes, cut their hair the same way, and want desperately to be part of the group. The desire to conform to a desirable group is so powerful that it can actually end up in cult-type behaviors.

Are you familiar with "thought-contagion"? This is the name for the type of strange behavior that occurs when a stadium full of out-of-control football fans begins to throw beer bottles onto the field. When one fan does it, suddenly it seems okay and more fans do it. There is also some deindividuation that takes place. Individual group members will begin to feel anonymous in the group yet compelled to act like the group, to belong and fit in.

Knowing that each of us has a hard-wired, biological need to belong and be part of the group can help us. We can use this knowledge to get our way, and at the same time help our targets get some of what they want.

For example, a conversation like this might take place at work: "You know, Bill, those of us in upper management don't normally give a project like this to someone at your level. But we believe you have the potential to become one of us. So, do your best work and we'll talk soon."

Or: "Once you have one of these, Mr. Prospect, everyone will know you have arrived! You'll be one of the most admired people around!"

Or: "When most people get the blue one, they also get the yellow and white ones as well."

In another setting you can see the need to be part of the collective at work: the hungry traveler. Imagine that you have been driving in your car for hours and you're getting hungry. You decide to take the next exit and get some dinner. When you exit, you see four places to eat, but each has an unfamiliar name. What do you do? You look for where the most cars are. You want to be safe and do what everyone else is doing. The power to conform is found in almost every single aspect of our lives.

Any attempt at showing what similar others have done is a powerful appeal to your targets because, fundamentally, they want to be just like everyone else.

COVERT PERSUASION TACTIC #27

Create Contrast

When two people, things, or places that are relatively different from each other are placed next to each other in time, space, or thought, we see them as very different, and it is easier to distinguish which one we want more. The question becomes "which" not "whether or not to."

People will, if given a choice between two things, choose the less expensive option. There is a funny example from *The Tonight Show* with Johnny Carson when he had the number-one Girl Scout cookie salesperson in the country on the show. He asked her the secret of her success. She said, "I just went to everyone's house and said, 'Can I have a $30,000 donation for the Girl Scouts?' When they said 'No,' I said, 'Would you at least buy a box of Girl Scout cookies?'"

The audience couldn't stop laughing. This little girl had mastered the art of contrast to help her sell—at age eight. You can use this too. Show your client the best option and/or the least expensive. The client is compelled to own something and normally will take the lease expensive item if it is shown last.

The same technique works in almost every setting in the business world. If you want someone to do something for you, simply ask him something you know he will never agree to, then, when he says no, ask him for the smaller favor. People will be more likely to help you after this small exchange than if you had asked for the smaller item first.

COVERT STRATEGY #4
Use "Postural Echo" to build instant rapport!
Do this:

Adopt a posture that is very similar to, but not exactly like, that of the person you wish to persuade. In addition, hold your arms in a very similar manner (but not exactly the same) as the person you want to persuade.

Done *covertly*, you can cause the other person to feel very willing to go along with your suggestions. The core psychological reason is that the target person feels that you are 'just like him'; therefore he begins to trust you implicitly.

This allows you almost instant trust and instant credibility. You will very soon be able to have this person do anything you want.

Note: There is a small warning with this trick. Be very subtle, because the moment the target person thinks you are copying him, all power is lost and you will not be successful at persuading this person.

COVERT PERSUASION TACTIC #28

Don't Ask "Why?" Because the Answer Is Meaningless

It's often a very big mistake to ask people why they decided to buy your product or service, vote for your candidate, or contribute to your cause. Why? Because people don't know why they do what they do. They simply cannot explain the reasons behind the decisions they make. But they will quickly tell you what they think you want to hear or something that makes them look good. But the truth, or the real core reasons, will never be known.

Because they don't know the answer to "why?", just don't ask the question. The key to success for you is to covertly deal with the subconscious mind while you persuade the conscious mind. Unless you have a very well planned strategy, don't ask why.

You'll be more successful when you analyze your own efforts and test one set of conditions against the control. The only vote that counts is if your target complies with your request. Ultimately, it is up to you to carefully analyze your own effort to determine what works and what doesn't. Don't trust the answers of your targets. They just don't know.

"The most valuable of all talents is that of never using two words when one will do."

—Thomas Jefferson

| **COVERT PERSUASION TACTIC #29** | **Shift Your Target's Time Reference** |

Shifting your target's time perspective helps him to make different decisions. Typically, soon after meeting you, your prospect will equate you with all the other people like you they have ever met and, draw some fast (probably false) conclusions about the value of what you represent.

You must do two things right away. First, distinguish yourself from all the other people like you they have ever met. Be original. Next, you must move their time filter from the past to the present, then into the future.

$10,000 COVERT PERSUASION TRICK

Did you know that when you have someone go into the future (in his mind) and think about going on a date with you, hiring you, or buying your product, that he will then think about what it is like to have done that? The best part is regardless of whether he thinks he will regret saying "yes" or not is almost irrelevant because the simple act of anticipating the outcome is enough to trigger the mind to say "Yes!"

COVERT PERSUASION TACTIC #30

Build Unshakable Credibility

An almost foolproof way to build credibility is to acknowledge the other person's (or other side's) point of view. Actually, adopt that position. Feel what he is feeling.

The other person will open up dramatically and be almost entirely defenseless. He will perceive you as interested in a fair and just outcome.

At this point, you can begin to assert your position or point of view and the other side will be much more receptive. Specifically, you do this by saying, "I used to feel the same way, until I found out that . . ." or, "I used to think that as well, but what I didn't know was . . ." An approach like this allows the other side to save face while adopting the new position you are asserting.

There are many other things that contribute to your credibility. For example, what are the sources for what you are saying? Does any generally recognized authority figure agree with, or already hold the position, you are advocating?

COVERT PERSUASION TRICK

Use the phrase, "You're right and _____."

"Kevin, you're right and that's what has worked for 20 years. Now the economy obviously is changing and you know what that means."

"You're right and _____" says what every one of us wants to hear. People go to all lengths to be right. Let people be right.

COVERT PERSUASION TACTIC #31	**Use Space as the Ultimate Covert Weapon**

There is a very specific art and science of using your environment and your place in it to persuade your target. This includes everything from what building or room you are in, to where you stand, and even how close to the other person you are.

Sometimes the use of space to help you persuade can be as simple as making sure you have home-field advantage. Simply having your target come to you and sit in *your* office can be very important. Sometimes the setting can be a powerful influence on the thinking and behavior of your target, even before you speak one word.

It's been said by many presidents of the United States that the Oval Office has a power all its own. It seems that when the biggest enemies of the president are summoned to the Oval Office, they walk through the door and are struck by the awesome environment. They are humbled by it. The power of their argument is weakened simply by the room they are standing in, and at the same time the president's position of power and his ultimate ability to persuade are increased many times over. All this happens *before* words are spoken.

Whether it's a single room or an entire building, some environ-

ments truly have a powerful sense of place. You'll immediately understand what this means by visiting some unique places. For example,
no matter what your particular religion may be, when you set foot
inside the National Cathedral in Washington, D.C., you know you
are in someplace special. You simply will not act the same way you do
when you're at home on a Sunday afternoon with friends watching
the big game on TV. The environment alone will have a huge impact
on your thoughts and behaviors.

Understanding this one principle will help you to be more
covertly persuasive because you can simply recommend that you
meet your target at a certain place and time. The suggestion will
have no significant meaning to your target (unless he has also read
this book). But when you thoughtfully choose the environment,
you are once step closer to getting your target to comply with
whatever you ask.

COVERT PERSUASION TACTIC #32	**Construct a Pattern of Commitment and Consistency**

You and I are more likely to make future decisions that are in line with similar past decisions.
Once we make a commitment to someone or something, our future actions will most likely be consistent with that previous commitment.

In selling, the first commitment is to get the appointment. Each
additional commitment may be very small, but you're building the
pattern of consistency that will lead to the final decision to buy
from you.

Ask your customers about the desire to enjoy the benefits of
what your product or service will ultimately supply (not your actual product or service; you're asking them to agree with you that

enjoying the end result is desirable). One way to do this is the simple question: "You would like to save over $3,000 per month, right?" Or "Tell me, if that happened this month, what would you do with that extra $3,000?" This causes them to agree that the savings would be nice to have, and it puts their focus on the future and gets them to mentally spend the savings on something they want. Now, when you mentally bring them back to the present and tie that desired result to your product or service, they are more likely to be consistent with their prior commitment and buy your product or service.

	Use Covert Hypnotic Language Patterns
COVERT PERSUASION TACTIC #33	There are very specific verbal tricks you can use to move the mind of the other person into the direction you desire.

The foundation of the Hypnotic Language Patterns is a term called "presupposition." This is the word for the intent that you are placing behind what you are saying. For example, if you say, "It's probably your ability to speed-read that allows you to learn so quickly." The presupposition in that sentence is that *something helps you to learn so quickly; it must be the fact that you can speed-read.*

Presuppositions are powerfully hypnotic and very covert. Very often the well-thought–out statement will include many presuppositions that the brain of the other person will pick up and subconsciously accept without any conscious scrutiny.

Here's another example: "*Before you work on that special report, let's grab a quick bite to eat, okay?*" This presupposes that the person will in fact work on that "special report." Did you notice the "*okay?*" at the end? That's a leading technique, and it is usually accompanied by an up and down nodding-yes motion of the head as it's asked. Many times the other person will easily comply with your request.

People who study hypnosis have discovered that there are many ways to get a person into a specific frame of mind and then get them to think about anything the hypnotist desires. Your goal is to get people to imagine the outcome you want (owning the product, enjoying the benefits of the service, voting for the candidate, helping on the project, and so forth).

Imagining something is often the first step toward getting it or avoiding it. Then we want them to tell us how they will go about buying our products and services or complying with our request to help accomplish whatever our goal is for the moment.

People will not give you these secret codes to their thinking just because you ask. You need to use the scientifically proven techniques in a very artful manner. There are specific words and phrases that yield amazing results in gaining compliance. Below are some of the phrases that have been shown to get a person to come to a conclusion that is all but predetermined.

You will notice that all the hypnotic language patterns are in bold face, and we assume that whatever follows the pattern will be acted upon. In other words, in the first example the hypnotic command is to "*buy this car, that's your decision.*" It follows the hypnotic sentence fragment, "**I wouldn't tell you to . . .**" All of the commands that follow are written in small capitals and the hypnotic language is in bold. A command is the specific action we want the client to take. Most of these patterns are not what would be considered good English or grammatically correct. *However, these patterns are very powerful and we recommend caution when using them.* Some brief but important comments follow in parentheses.

"**I wouldn't tell you to** BUY THIS CAR, that's your decision."

"**I wouldn't tell you to** INVEST MORE MONEY IN STOCKS; you need to figure that out on your own." (I wouldn't tell you, but notice that the command is still coming!)

$10,000 Covert Persuasion Trick

When you ask how they go about deciding, you learn specifically how they *believe* they decide and then they give you the specific instructions on how you can change their minds (and sell them, convince them, persuade them).

"**You might want to ____ now**, JOIN THE CLUB FOR ONLY ONE YEAR THEN RENEW."

"**You might want to ____ now**, BUY THIS BEAUTIFUL CAR."

(You don't *have to*, but you just might!)

"**What is it that helps you know whether you should** BUY AN X OR A Y?"

"**What is it that helps you know whether you** WANT TO UPGRADE **now** OR WAIT A WHILE?"

(Again, you are really asking for their specific decision strategy.)

"**You don't have to** DECIDE **now**."

"**You don't have to** INVEST IN SEVERAL FUNDS; ONE OR TWO IS JUST FINE." ("I will if I want to!")

"**Why is it that some people** JUST DON'T SEE THE VALUE OF OWNING A QUALITY CAR?"

"**Why is it that some people** JUST SEE GREATNESS AND IT ELUDES OTHERS?" (Not you Mr. Target, but *some people* . . .)

"**I don't know if** SIGNING UP **now** IS WHAT YOU WANT TO DO."

"**I don't know if** DECIDING **now** IS ABSOLUTELY NECESSARY SO YOU DON'T LOSE OUT." (Actually I do know, but I'm being very gentle.)

"**Would you like to see** A BIGGER HOUSE?"

"**Would you like to see** THIS IN BLUE?"

"**Would you like to have** OUR CLIENT SERVICES PEOPLE CALL YOU REGULARLY?" (You are asking for specific features and benefits that they might or might not want.)

"**Some people** ARE INVESTING A GREAT DEAL OF MONEY RIGHT **now**."

"**Some people** ARE SNAPPING UP HOUSES LIKE THEY ARE GOING OUT OF STYLE." ("Some people" is your target.)

"**If you could have** a PERFECT CAR, WHAT WOULD IT BE LIKE?"

"**If you could have** THE PERFECT SPEAKER FOR YOUR FUNCTION, WHAT WOULD HE BE LIKE?"

$10,000 COVERT PERSUASION TRICK
"If you could have . . ." = "imagine."

It goes straight to the subconscious mind and goes to work like a mind virus.

"**If you could choose** ANY MUTUAL FUND, WHAT QUALITIES WOULD YOU WANT IT TO HAVE?"

"**If you could choose** A BETTER INSURANCE COMPANY, WHAT **would** BE MOST IMPORTANT TO YOU?" (He can choose and his brain will tell him to choose it, now!)

"**Have you ever seen** A TRULY AMAZING SALES TRAINER?"

"**Have you ever seen** A SPEAKER THAT MOTIVATES THE DAY AFTER HE LEAVES?" (Again, this is the same as "imagine." It's a no-pressure question that darts through the brain at high speeds causing a "yes, I want it" response.")

"**Would you be surprised if I told you** THAT MOST PEOPLE AREN'T AS ASTUTE AS YOU ARE?"

"**Would you be surprised if I told you** THAT THIS CAR GETS 30 MPG?" ("Would you be surprised if I told you" implies you have the shocking truth.)

"**Imagine what would happen if** YOUR PORTFOLIO AVERAGED 12 PERCENT PER YEAR!"

"**Imagine what would happen if** YOU LIVED IN A HOUSE THAT YOU COULD REALLY BE PROUD OF!" (Once again, we have "imagine" lighting up the brain like a Christmas tree.)

"**Are you interested in** MAKING MORE MONEY SHORT TERM OR LONG TERM?"

"**Are you interested in** MAKING THE ONLINE EXPERIENCE FOR YOUR CLIENTS EASY AND FUN?" (He knows he should be interested, and now he has to say yes or pick which is best for him.)

"**If I could show you a way to** MAKE MORE MONEY, **would you** HIRE OUR FIRM?"

"**If I could show you a way to** LOOK 10 YEARS YOUNGER, WOULD YOU DO IT?" (This is a perfect, preclosing question. You wouldn't ask it unless you could show him, so now you get the "yes" response, and then you close after you show him.)

"**What would it be like if you had** AN EXTRA $25,000 PER YEAR IN INCOME?"

"**What would it be like if you had** A BODY THAT PEOPLE WOULD BE MAGNETIZED TO?" (Imagine that . . .)

"**You may not know** THAT THIS IS GOING TO BE FUN."

"**You may not know** THAT WE ARE GOING TO BE WORKING TOGETHER FOR A LONG TIME!" (He'll know right after you say, "You may not know . . .")

"**Can I show you** SEVEN WAYS TO INCREASE YOUR PERSONAL SALES?"

"**Can I show you** HOW TO WORK OUT IN SUCH A WAY THAT YOU WILL BE STRONGER AND LOOK BETTER?" (Getting permission to sell your client is kind and effective.)

"**I'm wondering if** DECIDING TODAY WILL MAKE YOU FEEL MORE COMFORTABLE INSIDE."

"**I'm wondering if** INVESTING TODAY IS GOING TO MAKE YOU THE MOST MONEY LONG TERM." (I'm wondering while you imagine.)

"**Don't you think that** IT'S TIME FOR A NEW PRESIDENT TO LEAD OUR COUNTRY?"

"**Don't you think that** A MUTUAL FUND THAT HAS A PROVEN TRACK RECORD IS BETTER THAN . . .?" (It's hard to say "no" to anything that follows, "Don't you think that . . .")

"**Don't you feel** THAT YOU ARE HAPPIER WHEN YOU HAVE SOMEONE DO YOUR TAXES FOR YOU?"

"**Don't you feel** THAT YOU ARE BETTER OFF WITH A NEW CAR THAN AN OLD ONE?"

Let's quickly recap these Hypnotic Language Patterns:

- I wouldn't tell you to . . .
- How do you go about deciding . . .
- You might want to now . . .
- What is it that helps you know whether you . . .
- You don't have to . . .
- Why is it that some people . . .
- I don't know if . . .
- Would you like to see . . .
- Some people . . .
- If you could have . . .
- If you would choose . . .
- Have you ever seen . . .
- Would you be surprised if I told you . . .
- Imagine what would happen if . . .
- Are you interested in . . .
- If I could show you a way to . . .
- What would it be like if you had . . .
- You may not know . . .
- Can I show you . . .
- I'm wondering if . . .
- Don't think that . . .
- Don't you feel . . .

Simply saying these phrases is no guarantee the other person will do what you want. Tonality, vocal pacing, variation, and content all matter too. Practice using these phrases in as many different work settings as possible and watch what happens. People will begin complying with more of your requests than they ever have in the past.

	Make Your Body Say What Your Words Say
COVERT PERSUASION TACTIC #34	When your entire body, mind, and message are all sending the same exact message out to your listener, you will be thousands of times more

persuasive. When even one tiny part of your total message delivery falters, your chances of persuading the other person to your way of thinking drop to almost zero.

In a famously misquoted study, Dr. Albert Mehrabian found that when pitting vocal cues against facial cues and the spoken word, the least important factor in the message was the words:

- 55% Facial cues
- 38% Vocal cues
- 7% Words

Notice that only 7 percent of the meaning and message in Mehrabian's experiment was carried to the listener through the actual words that were spoken. A much higher 38 percent of the meaning was delivered using vocal cues. And a shocking 55 percent of the entire intent and meaning was delivered by facial cues of study participants. Most people never stop to consider these three elements; however, these are the three that must all send the exact same message for you to have maximum persuasion power.

It takes active thought on your part to put together a 100 percent congruent message. Most people never take the time to work on all three points, and that's exactly why most people are not very persuasive. Or if they do happen to persuade someone, they have no idea why they were successful. But now that you know this formula, you'll be 100 percent effective when you choose to be.

The key to success in delivering a 100 percent congruent message is to think through the entire presentation and delivery of your message. Carefully choose the actual words you will use, and then practice out loud exactly how you will say it. In fact, go one step further and get out a tape recorder and tape what you are saying as you practice. Then play it back. You may be shocked. This is a great tool because when you audiotape yourself, you are only hearing the words you are saying and how you are saying them. It effectively isolates and eliminates the impact of most body language cues that are present in the communication. And finally, thoughtfully work on your body language. The best feedback here is to videotape yourself making the presentation. You'll be surprised how different it is to watch yourself.

If you're unsure how to improve your body language, you're in luck because there is an entire chapter in this book on the power of your body language, complete with tips to improve the power of your presence so that you are many times more persuasive.

	Think Like a Jedi. . . . Use OBT
COVERT PERSUASION TACTIC #35	**(Outcome-Based Thinking)**

Do you remember the trick to working those mazes in children's books? Do you remember how much easier they were when you discovered that starting from the end and working backwards toward the "start" worked much easier? Well, outcome-based thinking is a lot like starting where you want to end up and working backwards toward where you are now. This will almost certainly assure that you arrive at the outcome you are looking for. OBT is useful in achieving the spectrum of very short-term outcomes to very long term because of its flexibility.

A great example of an outcome-based thinker is any one of the athletes on an Olympic team. They achieve top performance in their sport (and win Olympic gold) by calmly, vividly, and repeatedly visualizing the flawless execution and perfect finish of their particular sport.

Similarly, the world's best salespeople and business people visualize their desired outcome with the same rich clarity. This helps them to properly prepare for every eventuality and increase their likelihood of success.

How do you know what outcome you *really* want? Do the following exercise; it may provide you with some greater, deeper, and truer insights into exactly what you want.

Get a pen, some paper, and go to a place where you are sure not to be interrupted. Then, ask yourself the following question: "*What dreams do I have for my life in regard to relationships, business, career, family, friends, income, and retirement?*"

Next, write a sentence or two about why you want each of these things and what they will mean to you when you have them. If you can't find a couple of sentences for a certain item, cross it completely off your list for now. Then, write a number next to the dreams that remain. Write a 1, 5, 10, or 20 depending on how much time it will take to realistically accomplish the goal. Finally, write a couple of sentences about what can come between you and your goal.

Now, choose your number one goal to begin working on. Then imagine the scene of your first encounter with the other person and ask yourself the following questions:

1. What precisely do I want out of the process?
2. What does the other person want? If I don't know, what is he likely to want?
3. What is the least I will accept out of the process?

4. What problems could come up in the process?

5. How will I deal with each one and, if possible, use the problem as a benefit for the other person?

6. How will I bring the process to a conclusion?

All master persuaders use this process, whether they are conscious of it or not.

When this process is followed, magic happens. To the people who do not have any understanding of Covert Persuasion it will just seem like you are lucky. But you'll know the real reason why. It all starts with very conscious, very hard work. You will have prepared yourself well for the opportunity when it comes. And, as you've heard, "Luck is when preparation meets opportunity." When you use outcome-based thinking, you'll be ready to reach your goals very efficiently and with the willing and eager cooperation of others.

"All that you accomplish or fail to accomplish with your life is the direct result of your thoughts."

—James Allen

COVERT **PERSUASION** **TACTIC #36**	**Determine How People Represent Information—to Themselves and to You**

There are three primary modalities that we use to take in most of our information. First there is the visual. This is everything we see. Our visual world is often "proof" of something—we'll believe it when we see it! Often when persuading another person, it helps to include powerful visual aides in your attempt.

Visual evidence adds power and credibility to your effort. You'll know people use their visual channel as their primary method of proof when they say things like "It's crystal clear to me," and "Okay, I can picture that," or "I see what you mean."

Second, there is the auditory channel. When someone tells us something, or we hear something we think is important, we are using our auditory channel. You'll know your target is primarily auditory when he says things like "That sounds about right," or "That doesn't ring any bells for me," and "That clicks for me."

Finally, there is the kinesthetic channel. This is where feelings enter the picture ("entering the picture" is a visual indicator—did you catch that). When a person primarily proves things with feelings, he will say things like "It just doesn't *feel* right" or "I feel good about that."

This technique becomes a covert weapon by listening closely to your targets. By listening closely to the words they use, you'll be given clues to how they primarily process information. Then, simply use that same channel when making your persuasive request. For example, you may hear your target say, "You know, I really like the sound of that." It can be as simple as responding to your target with something like "Well, when you use this model, your whole production system will just begin to click." Using this type of auditory language will be very persuasive with this particular person. You're really speaking his language and he will be more receptive to you and your requests.

| **COVERT PERSUASION TACTIC #37** | **FFF Technique** |

FFF Technique

The Feel, Felt, Found technique has been used in the sales field for a long time; however, like most great persuasion techniques, it truly has applications in every single area of life. This one is special and is very, very effective because it works on a couple of different levels.

Here's an example of this technique at work: "*I understand how you **feel** about that, many of my customers once **felt** the very same way, but when they looked closer, they **found** . . .*" If you're not in sales, you can slightly change that middle "felt" so that it's: "*many others have **felt***".

There are several reasons this technique is so valuable. First, it works at the level of empathy. This is an emotional connection to your targets and often completely bypasses the critical side of their brains. When it's stated with sincere empathy, it works. If you fake it, you will fail.

Next, the technique goes on to say that *many similar others* have **felt** the same way. This lets them know that they're not alone. People like to know that other people just like them have done the same thing. This is a simple and direct way of providing "social proof" that others have done this also. This takes risk away. It makes your targets feel more comfortable.

Finally, you help them share in the discovery of the solution. When you say, "*but when they looked closer, they **found**,*" you allow them to save face. This is a critical step because it makes it okay to make a decision in your favor based on this new fact.

COVERT PERSUASION TACTIC #38

Deletion, Distortion, and Generalization

We all do this, every single day and it shortens and neutralizes communication to the point of being ineffective. Sounds encouraging? Don't worry, because once you realize what it is, you can control when and to what degree you do it.

First is *Deletion*. We do this out of necessity; otherwise we would be describing every detail of every single thing all the time. Life is too short, and the attention span of the person we're attempting to persuade is drastically shorter, so we leave out some unimportant details. But, now for the first time, we're going to ask you to think carefully about what you leave out. All too often, people leave out very important and potentially very persuasive details that could help persuade the other person.

Next is *Distortion.* "It was the worst movie of all time! It lasted like 4 hours! And the special effects? They looked like my 8-year-old nephew did them at home!" Okay, I distorted the facts a little there, but I think you get the point. Sometimes just to make a point we will distort some aspects of a story or situation. But even on a subconscious level we often distort reality to ourselves and when we describe things to others. Distortion happens and sometimes it helps, but often it hurts. So, watch your distortions closely.

Finally, there is *Generalization.* Everybody does it, all the time, and it impacts every single part of everyone's life. I generalized things a little there, but I think you get the point.

Knowing the power of these three filters, we can use them to delete the things in our proposal that our target would object to, distort the benefits and the losses, and generalize the overall outcome so that it's in our target's favor. Know that we all delete, distort, and generalize and use this to your advantage by helping people to do these things in the direction and amount that will make your request most appealing to them.

	The Note-Taking Tactic
COVERT PERSUASION TACTIC #39	There are times when it's very important that you make sure your target actually sticks to the decision he makes to go along with you and take

the action you're requesting. To make sure targets follow through, get them to write it down.

Why does this work? The covert power behind this commitment technique comes from its ability to directly and actively involve your targets. Getting them to write down that they will do a certain thing dramatically increases the chances of their actually doing it. The act of writing is a form of commitment.

During your persuasion attempt, be sure to put a pen in the hand of your target. Then, at the right time, get him involved with writing out the solution. Have him sketch what the solution would look like. Have him write out what the ultimate benefit would be to himself if everything you're promising comes true. Have him write down how complying with your request will make him look in the eyes of his superiors. Write it all down. The more that gets written, the stronger the commitment will be and the more likely he will take the action you want.

When persuading, don't forget the covert tools of pen and paper.

COVERT PERSUASION TACTIC #40

Lower Your Voice at the Right Moment

This is a little known technique. It's most effective when trying to communicate authority and confidence. You can say the exact same sentence; simply lower your voice (pitch/tone), and you'll be perceived as more credible and sometimes more powerful. The difficult part of this technique is maintaining total and complete control of yourself during the exchange.

Listen carefully to the nightly TV news. The anchor will have a way of lowering the voice to impart a tone of seriousness and authority. Then when switching to a lighter human-interest story, anchors will change their voice to let you know this is lighter material and possibly funny. Listen carefully to your local or national TV news anchor. They are professionals at delivering meaning by using tone, pitch, and range of their voices. We can learn a lot from watching TV.

When you have the mental control to stay on-task and on-message, you will free up your ability to control this subtle but powerful part of your presence.

"The human voice is the organ of the soul."

—Henry Wadsworth Longfellow

COVERT PERSUASION TACTIC #41	**80/20 Rule Covert Persuasion**

Because you are in the business world, you are certainly aware of the 80/20 Rule. Put simply, 80 percent of your results will come from 20 percent of your efforts. This rule applies to almost everything in your professional and personal life.

Sometimes this is referred to as the Pareto Principle, after Italian economist Vilfredo Pareto. He discovered that 20 percent of the people in his time owned 80 percent of the land and the assets of the country.

Today this concept has been spread to almost every area of your life and is generally true across categories and countries. Look at these interesting examples of the 80/20 rule:

- 20% of the menu items of the average restaurant account for 80% of the revenue.
- 20% of the new car models account for 80% of the sales.
- 20% of the customers account for 80% of the sales.

When you are crafting your approach to your target, realize that success will come more often from using a combination of a couple of the covert persuasion tactics and tricks you find in this book. In other words, you'll get about 80 percent of your successes from using

20 percent of the techniques and tricks in this book. Sometimes it's more important to use a few techniques or tricks with a very high degree of skill than it is to simply try to use a huge number of them. That can sometimes backfire.

Knowing the 80/20 rule will help you become a more efficient and skillful persuader.

COVERT PERSUASION TACTIC #42	### Inoculation to Persuade Your Prospect and Reduce Buyer's Remorse

Peer pressure doesn't end in high school. We are often *very* concerned with what other people think about our purchases or choices. Sometimes after your targets have made the decision you wanted them to make, it doesn't stick, and they end up changing their minds. Why? Simply, they talked to other people who have power and influence in their lives and those people told them they were wrong. So they contact you and change their decision.

The process is similar to a flu virus that changes your state from healthy to sick. You can think of the other brains your targets will come in contact with as infectious viruses. Your job is to "inoculate" them against these mind viruses so the decisions they made in your favor do not change. In fact, if you are skillful with this technique, the actions and reactions of others will tend to strengthen the original decision of your target.

Because you have completely thought through what your target will likely say to you in response to your persuasion effort, you can also predict what others will say to your target afterwards. Anything you can predict, you can prepare for in advance.

Let's assume that after you've been successful and secured a commitment to comply with you, your target runs into others at work that will try to change his mind. Let's look at how we can "inoculate" them.

Because you know to expect resistance, you can share this expectation with your target. It might sound something like this: "You and I both know this is the right decision because we know all the facts. But what will you say to those who wonder why you're doing this and try to change your mind?"

That question does a lot of things. First of all, it puts you and your target on the same side. When you say, "*You and I both know*" you're on the same team; you share a common understanding. Then, we say that the decision is right "*because we know all the facts*." This is very powerful because we've used the word "because." As discussed earlier, the word because is like a magic mind trigger that immediately gives reason and grounding to a decision. Then, we mention that we know all the facts. This changes what up to this point might be a very emotion-based decision into a fact-based decision. Nothing has really changed except the word labels we place on what's happening. We end with a direct question, which asks your target to defend the decision he have just made right back to us. This is a practice round, sort of role-playing for what you expect in the future. When targets answer that question, they have been inoculated against other forces that are around them when you're not. This gives a much greater degree of certainty that they will be consistent with this commitment to comply with your request and help you reach your goal. It works!

When your targets agree with your request, but seems somewhat hesitant, use this technique to inoculate them and make them stick to the decision they've just made. Ask the important question: "*You and I both know this is the right decision because we know all the facts. But what will you say to those who wonder why you're doing this and try to change your mind?*" This technique works because the use of the question allows it to fly right by the critical mind. The best way to understand this technique is to actually use it. Ask this question to inoculate your target and you'll see its power.

COVERT
PERSUASION
TACTIC #43

Flexibility

Sometimes being the most persuasive person means being the most flexible. Flexibility is key, not only in the tactics or tricks you employ to get your way, but also in the path you take to get to your goal.

Just imagine that the bridge is out on your way to work tomorrow morning. What would you do? It's a good bet you wouldn't just sit there. It's also a safe bet you wouldn't just turn around and go back home and go to bed. No, instead, you would take side streets you normally don't use, and you would creatively find an alternate route to your destination.

The same is true of persuasion attempts. Sometimes even though we spend time thinking through our approach and all anticipated reactions, our efforts still fail. However, failure is not final until you agree that it is. So, the best solution is to pretend the "bridge is out" and creatively find another way to approach your target person. Notice your goal has not changed at all. You're still achieving the same end but just using different means. This is the flexibility technique in action.

Make a big list of all the covert persuasion techniques that might apply in your situation. This becomes your road map. Then, when some roads are blocked, simply get out your map and choose another one.

Think of how kids ask for what they want. They are persistent. They will ask, ask, and ask again. Sometimes they will ask in the same way, but very often they will be highly creative in asking for what they want. Sometimes they will even bargain for it. They may make certain promises or guarantee to do chores. They have their sights set on a certain thing and they are not going to give up until they exhaust every single possibility.

When we adopt this attitude of persistence and commit to maintaining a flexible approach, we will succeed more often than we fail in this game of persuasion.

Covertly Empathetic Mind

COVERT PERSUASION TACTIC #44

There are literally dozens of qualities necessary for consistently succeeding at Covert Persuasion; however, there is one that is so powerful it dwarfs all the others. What is it? *Empathy!* You may be saying wait a minute, empathy as a technique? Yes.

The ability to empathize with others is critical. If your target doesn't see you as empathetic and genuinely and sincerely caring, your persuasion attempt will fail. This is true every single time. To prove this, think about the opposite scenario of your client seeing you as fake, uncaring, and possibly even manipulative. No one in his or her right mind would willingly cooperate with someone that was viewed in that manner. They must see you as empathetic, genuine, and trustworthy or they will see you as a risk. This is really a "yes" or "no" type of situation.

What is empathy? It's the ability to understand, to see things from other people's point of view, to walk a mile in their shoes. When you can do this and, more importantly, when the other person perceives you in this light, you will be instantly more effective at persuading him to your way of thinking.

What you are truly doing is asking other people to believe in you. You are selling yourself first and your idea, cause, or candidate second.

To convey empathy covertly, you must genuinely have the real interests of your targets in mind. One sure-fire way to clearly communicate that to your targets is to ask questions that get them talking about what it is they want. For example, "It seems to me that you really care about what happens next, can you tell me more about that?" A question like this will get them to tell you the material you need to turn that phrasing back around and allow them to easily see that you genuinely care about the same outcome they do. It may sound like this, "I understand, I feel the same way. I agree with you that is the most important. Since we agree on this, let's work together to get it done. The first step then is obviously X, would you like to do X or Y?" Obviously, the action you request will ultimately lead your targets to your goal, while at the same time appearing to help advance them toward theirs.

COVERT PERSUASION TACTIC #45	**Artfully Vague Language**

Artfully Vague Language

When using this technique, think of politicians; they have almost mastered this one. The idea is to say something that means nothing but sounds like something. Why? Simply because your goal is to allow the other person to assign their own personal meaning to the words you're using to send your message.

For example, "*Our entire tax system needs reforming in this country.*" That sentence literally means nothing. Every single person hearing it can draw his own conclusion, and then sincerely believe that the candidate has his best interests at heart. Sometimes it's that shockingly simple. From a statement like that, a skilled politician may be able to persuade people to vote for him. Amazing isn't it?

Another example of people that use artfully vague language is those who write horoscopes in the newspaper. It really does seem as if they say something. But if you look at them objectively, they say nothing. Some people read them daily and then infuse those words with specific meaning in their own lives. The vague language will be converted into a specific meaning that is true for them! They will then come to believe in the power of the horoscopes. Watch these little predictions of the future long enough, and you'll see virtually the same predictions cycle through all the astrological signs.

This technique usually works best when persuading a group. For example, when you're giving a speech or formal presentation of some kind and you want the audience to agree with you, the skillful use of artfully vague language will allow people to derive their own specific meaning out of what you said, and ultimately they'll feel supportive of your position. The key is to use general words that are common to all positions and then allow your targets to assign their own specific meaning.

I had the privilege of having lunch with the chairman of the board of one of the nation's largest steel companies. I introduced him to the audience of selected business owners and leaders from a wide variety of enterprises. During his remarks, he spoke briefly about the current lack of and the real need for ethics and integrity in business. The chairman went on to say that without this strong moral foundation for a business, it will fail. Without a strong unbending ethical core, tragedies like WorldCom and Enron happen.

The hundreds of heads in the room were nodding in agreement with the speaker. After he finished speaking, several in the audience asked me to get copies of his speech so they could take these core thoughts on success based on ethics and integrity back to their own companies.

This is a great example of artfully vague language that motivated others to act to make their own situation and ultimately the world a better place. Artfully vague language, delivered skillfully, can move people to positive action. And, of course, it does so covertly.

COVERT PERSUASION TACTIC #46

Power of Three

Have you ever noticed that many arguments come with a trilogy of words built in? It's probably the most often used, most persuasive, and successful approach you can use. (Did you notice that the previous sentence had three parts?)

The key here is to put three presuppositions in a row. The technique is a way of creating "controlled overwhelm" in the mind of your target. You want to communicate just enough to cause a little bit of confusion in his mind. The goal is to include one item in your triad that is very obviously true. Then, your target's mind will expand its acceptance of the other two ideas in your triad, thinking that if that one thing is true, the other two are likely to be true as well.

Psychologists generally agree that we have the ability to sort through the meanings of up to three presuppositions in a conversation; however, if we include more than three, it moves beyond the brain's search capabilities. Since the brain is a pattern-seeking, efficient operator, it will quickly try to determine if one is true, then, in most cases, conclude that all are true. That's how you get compliance.

For example, in your prework while crafting your approach, you'll want to write down the end states you want your target to be feeling. Knowing what that goal is, what presuppositions will have to be true to lead your target in that direction?

Let's say you want your target to feel "confident"; it would be a good idea to fill up an entire sheet of paper with all the presuppositions you can think of about "confidence." Then include three in your compact argument. Make sure that two are designed to stretch the mind of your prospect in the direction you want it to go, but give him one that he can obviously and quickly agree is completely true. This technique causes the brain to think that if that one item is true, so are the rest of them. In other words, you'll enjoy a successful persuasion outcome.

> *"If you can't convince them, confuse them."*
>
> —Harry S. Truman

Vocal Stress in Delivery

COVERT PERSUASION TACTIC #47

This technique is difficult to convey on the printed page, but we'll do our best. Tonal marking is accomplished by changing your pitch and skillfully pausing for impact while you make your point.

The very best way to practice this technique is to write out the sentences you plan on saying. Then take a highlighter and highlight the imbedded commands you want to stress. Finally, read these sentences out loud into a tape recorder. Do this over and over until you can say the lines confidently and smoothly. Then take a break. Walk away. Let as much time pass as you can. When you return, play that tape back and ask yourself if *you* would be convinced by your argument, position, or request. Be honest; would you be persuaded by you? Sometimes we are our own harshest critic.

Vocal stress occurs when the tone of your voice conveys much more meaning than the words themselves. When you combine this power of vocal stress with commands, questions, and statements, there is maximum persuasive power on the tip of your tongue.

Commands are generally said with a downturn emphasis. Questions are read with a rising emphasis at the end. Statements are generally read flat.

For example, take any sentence and read it, vocally stressing a different word each time, and you'll convey completely different meanings. Let's try it with this; "I didn't know he offended the client."

When you say, "*I* didn't know he offended the client," you're excusing yourself from the incident.

When you say, "I didn't *know* he offended the client," you're saying you had a pretty good idea that's what happened, but you didn't *know* it for sure.

When you say, "I didn't know *he* offended the client," you're saying that you are aware that the client was offended, but you weren't aware that *he* is the one who did it.

And finally, when you say, "I didn't know he offended the *client*," you're acknowledging that you know he offended someone; you're just not sure it was the client.

From this quick example, you can see that the place you put the vocal stress will have a huge impact on the meaning you are convey-ing. If your upcoming persuasion encounter is important, I strongly recommend writing out what you're going to say and practicing *how* you're going to say it. Know exactly where you want to put the vocal stress. If you leave this to chance, you're leaving the entire meaning up to chance, and you can't afford to do that.

COVERT PERSUASION TACTIC #48

Experiential Involvement

When you involve your targets with the process or experience of your goal in an active way, it forces their body language into a com-pliance mode. It's a generally accepted fact that when you get a person's body (or even mind) to move in the direction that's most helpful to your goal, he will begin agreeing and complying with your requests.

There are many ways to get bodies to move. If you're in business and you need the other person's cooperation to organize a large meeting or event, you may start with asking them to help you move some chairs from one area to another. The physical act of moving a couple of chairs will involve them to the point where they will begin to take some ownership of the event. This will make future requests for help regarding this project much more successful.

If you're in sales, getting the customer or prospect involved is critical. I remember that, when I was selling radio advertising, I would deliberately make a mistake or two on the proposed copy of the commercial, so the customers could get their pens out and cor-rect the copy. As small as this sounds, it involved them. They began to feel ownership of the project and it started conversation that led to more sales.

When you get your targets involved in the experience, they will comply with your requests much more often. It sounds almost too simple to work, but it does.

I have given a talk on the power of a persuasive attitude, and as part of it I have everyone stand up, raise one arm, point their index finger toward the ceiling, repeat the process with the other hand, and then smile as big as they can. I then tell them to look around the room. Everyone is usually laughing pretty heartily at this point. Then I tell them to, without changing anything at all, be depressed. It cannot be done. Why? Because when your body is in motion and doing something positive, it controls and directs your thoughts in the same way. I've proven that by active involvement I can control people's state of mind.

Always remember that involvement will persuade them very quickly and covertly.

$10,000 COVERT PERSUASION TRICK

People will comply with your requests more often and with more energy and commitment when you involve them in the experience. This activity gets their body involved first, and their mind will follow.

COVERT PERSUASION TACTIC #49	**Persuading with Attitude**

Your attitude has everything to do with your success as a professional persuader. Everything? Yes. It all starts with you. When you are totally in control of your own attitude and have made sure that it is positive and proactive, then you will have a much higher likelihood of successfully persuading your target.

This technique starts within you and then transfers, like a virus, to the mind of your target. You can think of it as a transfer of ideas, concepts, and suggestions for action. When successful, your target will share the exact same level of commitment and excitement you currently have. How do you covertly persuade with attitude?

There is a factor you can call "positive expectancy" that will determine your end result more often than not. Put simply, if you fully expect to be successful, then you most likely will be. This wordless thought contagion will infect the mind of your targets. They will absorb your attitude and reflect it back to you. Knowing this is true, and it is, it would seem to be simple to guide and control your own attitude so others would adopt it as well from simply being around you.

In order to make this a technique that you can choose to use every single day, you must commit to protecting your own mind. You can't let just any old thought enter. Think of the way the old forts were protected. They had big walls and soldiers with guns. Build that same wall around your brain. Be very selective about what you allow in. When you protect your own thoughts from the negative and bitter thoughts of others, you'll almost immediately become the type of person that others enjoy being around. You'll exude a real sense of confidence and you will have a noticeable sense of certainty that people will want to follow and support.

Commit to improving your attitude and protecting your mind from anything that takes energy away from your goals. Your improved attitude will be a contagious force that others will spring into action to support.

COVERT PERSUASION TACTIC #50

Using Music to Persuade

This particular technique is fascinating to me. We discuss the use of music in a couple of the stories in this book; however, we never really say why it works. Music has a biological connection to the mind and body that no one can fully explain.

It's interesting that we will listen to our favorite song or CD over and over again but only go to a seminar, a training session, or read a book once. Why do we listen to music? What is it about music that connects with us?

That's a huge question, and we don't have the room to completely cover a topic that big, but we can concentrate on a couple of specific types of persuasion that invade our lives every day with sound, rhythm, and beat. Can you think of times and places when sound and music guide your thinking and behavior?

One such area is radio jingles. You'll hear dozens every single day. Do they help persuade you to buy? Yes! Millions of dollars are spent every year on creating those precious seconds of musical memory pegs. They work. What other areas are there where music can play a role in our persuasion attempts?

- On-hold music: during the holiday season, classical holiday music helps to calm shoppers and put them in a buying mood.

- In-store music: background music helps move people at a certain pace; slow music = slow pace.

- At-work music: an up-tempo selection will help to brighten your day and make it move smoothly.

If possible, include music in your persuasion effort. From playing faster music in the background of a meeting that you want to continue moving along at a good pace, to creating a jingle for your product or service, music is a powerful persuader. Include it where appropriate and you'll notice the attention of your prospects will increase and ultimately, they will comply with you more often.

COVERT PERSUASION TACTIC #51

Inconsistency

After making perceived progress in some way, a person becomes more likely to do contrary behaviors. The person who lost 10 pounds is quite likely to celebrate with a milk shake or piece of cake. The person who makes a donation is likely to splurge on himself or herself. The person who just opened a retirement account is more likely to buy a new car.

Knowing that people are likely to behave inconsistently in these types of situations may provide you with the opportunity to covertly persuade them in the direction that helps you most.

For example, you may say, "Congratulations on your accomplishment—now don't you think it's time to reward yourself?" This is a great lead-in to persuading the person to go on that vacation, buy that expensive meal, or treat himself to that new car. The action you are helping them to take is the one that will help you the most.

COVERT PERSUASION TACTIC #52

Fewer Choices Means You'll Hear Yes More

People like to sample from variety, but they actually buy from only a few choices. An amazing amount of research has been done on this and it has been proved every time. One example involves those free samples at the grocery store.

In one experiment, the store offered many choices of jelly to taste. Lots of shoppers sampled the jelly, but few bought. In the other scenario, only a few samples were available to be tasted, but more people bought the jelly. Less choice produces higher gross sales.

The same principle holds true in many areas of your life. Take buying a car, for example. How many color choices are available, six or seven? Choosing a color becomes very easy. In another setting, say picking out paint colors for your walls, you have literally thousands of colors to choose from. In that type of decision, choosing becomes difficult and takes far more time.

The mind can easily go into overload. Beginning salespeople are taught not to "over talk" the sale. If they do they run the risk of "talking themselves out of a sale." There is such a thing as too much information. This information overload is directly responsible for confusion. And what do people do when they're confused? Right, they do nothing! They will generally freeze in their tracks. No decision. Or, at worst, they will become extremely conservative and decide not to spend the money. The answer to buy from or otherwise comply with you becomes "no!"

Therefore, when choices are available to your targets, limit the number of them and you'll increase the chances they will take the action you want.

$10,000 COVERT PERSUASION TRICK

When you are covertly persuading another person to go along with you, cut back on the total number of choices available to them. When you do this, it's much more likely they will go along with you.

COVERT PERSUASION TACTIC #53

People Believe What They Say, Not What You Say

You know this is true. Think about it from your own point of view. Whenever someone tried to tell you something, you instinctively push back, right? This "push back" usually happens when someone tries to convince someone else by telling him what to do or how to decide.

We all like to decide for ourselves. We like to come to our own conclusions about the situations in our lives. We like to be in control. We do not like to be told what to do. There is a hit to the self-esteem when that happens to us as adults.

Therefore, the best way to bring the other person to the predetermined outcome that you're looking for is to *ask* questions that involve the other person. But, as all good lawyers know, never ask a question whose answer will not take you toward your goal. In other words, you must know the answer *before* you ask the question.

However, the simple act of answering your question allows your targets to draw their conclusions independently. Whether they say something to you aloud in response, or simple answer silently in their own heads, that is the voice they will listen to—their own. Knowing this will allow you to construct the question you ask so that the answer you want is the most likely response.

COVERT PERSUASION TACTIC #54

Be Private in Public and You Will Be More Successful

This is among the best advice I have ever been given. This advice has made me "real" and approachable by all the audiences I've ever had the privilege to speak to. When the real, human side of me is able to shine, there is a solid and profound mental and emotional connection with everyone in my audience.

People want to know that you are real. They want to know that you have felt pain. They want to know that you deeply understand them and have real experiences to share with them that can have a positive, powerful, and lasting impact on their lives.

This technique generally works best when persuading more than one person to go along with you. Whether a small meeting in your company or with your committee, or even in front of hundreds of people, the same private core communicator must come out. Share those quick, but personal, stories about how you were once in an awkward situation and were able to find your way out of it.

Covertly, the mind of your targets will identify with you and your genuineness. They will feel that they are just like you. This type of covert bond will allow your targets' defenses to lower just enough that your new ideas can enter and take hold.

COVERT PERSUASION TACTIC #55	**Oscillation at the Decision Point** There is typically an arbitrary decision point that is set in almost every negotiation, communication, or decision.

"I have to know today."
"If we don't have a deal by the 31st, I let someone else have it."
"If you buy today you get 10% off."

A decision needs to be, or probably will be, made. In some cases, if an obvious decision isn't instantly made (Yes, I will pull over for the police officer because I don't want this ticket to be higher than it is now), things could get worse. Almost all decisions that require conscious thought—most decisions require no thought or conscious attention at all—find people oscillating back and forth as to what to do, especially before the decision point.

Realize that people will make a very different decision at 5:00 P.M. than at 5:05 P.M. on something that goes back and forth a lot in their minds. People literally change their minds as each moment passes, in many decisions. Unless people have firm beliefs, they are constantly oscillating, sometimes with varying degrees of intensity. "No, absolutely not." That was today. Then tomorrow: "Well maybe." Then the next day: "I don't think so, but it's possible."

You can almost see the pendulum swing back and forth, or the child on the swing go higher or lower. More important for our dis-

cussion is that oscillation is not a day-to-day experience. It is a mo-
ment-to-moment experience. "Yes" and "no" in varying degrees flip-
flop from moment to moment and minute to minute.

The oscillation will continue indefinitely unless a new stimulus
enters the equation, and then any change is subject to further change.

Does Persuasion Change Behavior?

Once persuaded to do anything, there is definitely short-term
change in behavior. Instead of doing one thing, a person does another. Instead of believing one thing, a person believes another. Nevertheless, people can and do regularly change even strong beliefs. The
more public a person is with his belief/behavior, the more likely he is
to maintain that belief. (The minister of the church is more likely to
maintain his belief than the parishioner sitting in row 30 because of
the weekly public exposition of his beliefs through sermons and
prayers.)

Beliefs and behaviors that are not made public are more likely to
change from future attempts at persuasion.

Someone who begins a diet plan and attends classes or meetings
is likely to continue to succeed while attending the classes. As soon as
the person stops attending the classes or going to the meetings, the
chances are greatly increased that he will stop the weight control
program and revert to old behaviors.

The more public and the more important other people's opinions about a person are, the more powerful the desire one has to keep
the new belief or behavior.

Is There Anything We Can Reliably Predict Will Happen after a Person Has Been Persuaded?

Yes. For example, once someone has been persuaded, there is a very
good chance he will go through oscillations of regret, sometimes so

great that he will actually immediately change his mind again and cancel a purchase or not take a job he thought he should.

How Do You Deal with Regret?

You can virtually eliminate this specific reaction through the utilization of principles that allow people to anticipate their regret prior to the decision point so that when they experience the change of belief/behavior, they will expect it and react in a less intense fashion.

Did the firefighters need to be persuaded on 9/11 to rush in to the building? Did they experience oscillation?

You hire an accountant to do your books and reduce your taxes. Your personal trainer's job is to get rid of your gut. The chef? To cook. A police officer? To protect public safety.

But what happens when an airplane flies into a building? What happens inside the mind of the firefighter who is racing upstairs while everyone else is going down?

Specifically, there is no way to know. Even those firefighters who lived report what they think they remembered and thought at the time of the most incredible crisis imaginable. This is reminiscent of D-Day in some ways. The firefighter trains for disasters, but he usually has a sense of control about his own safety. Going into the World Trade Center was quite another thing.

We know that many individuals who were about to jump out a window and take their own lives called loved ones first. The same was true for passengers on the flight that was heroically downed in Pennsylvania that fateful day. We do know that oscillation probably takes place in these extraordinary circumstances. The desire to be with loved ones. The desire to live. Being able to live your life in the way you choose and ultimately die doing that which you love. I imagine there was oscillation, and I imagine it was fairly rapidly dismissed by the objective. Veterans of war no doubt experienced similar feelings, thoughts, and oscillations.

But what about the more mundane? Buying a car? Saying "yes" or "no" to the request for a date? Saying "yes" or "no" to the marriage proposal?

Time Perception and Feelings of Regret

There is ample evidence that reveals that the closer one comes to a goal or an objective (the wedding day, for example) the more likely we are to experience regret.

As humans, we experience a fear and anxiety response when we lose the "freedom options." As soon as a decision is near, anxiety can incapacitate a person, even on little decisions about what to eat in a restaurant.

In fact, there are reams of research that indicate an increased repulsion to the goal as it is approached. This often leads to self-sabotage and other destructive behaviors. This is why people say they would like to invest in their 401K plan next year, but if they had to make a deposit today they would not do so.

Secrets of Oscillation

Oscillation is not indecisiveness, per se. It is a normal and often useful reaction to situations that have unknown variables.

- Oscillation is wavering between two or more possibilities.
- The wavering can become more intense as the "deadline" looms.
- The anxiety and fear level increases as the deadline comes closer.
- The desire to move away from any choice that limits future freedom of choice in any way increases as a decision point nears.

A woman who is in love with two men chooses man "A." (Men do not choose women, regardless of what religion or theory of evolution you subscribe to that tells you otherwise.) She decides, "I will spend my life with Andrew." But as she comes closer and closer to actually spending the rest of her life with Andrew, she begins to wonder if she has made a big mistake and starts to seriously reconsider Bill. Sure, she dumped Bill a month ago, but really, when she thinks about it, Bill is probably the better choice.

Oscillation and the Sexes

This oscillation doesn't just happen with women. My mother regularly told me that "It's a woman's prerogative to change her mind." I always thought that was a lousy excuse. It turns out to be true, except that everyone changes his mind. Most people change their mind as the goal approaches, or as the other options are rejected.

Sometimes these oscillations are manifest in behavior. Sometimes they are not. Either way, they are happening in the mind of the individual.

When you are persuading your target, realize there is a real conversation happening inside his mind. He is going back and forth regarding the decision to comply with you. You need to strike, or ask the commitment question, when he is oscillating in your favor. Then, at that point bring some of the other covert persuasion techniques into play, such as inoculation, commitment and consistency, and involvement.

We've put this quick-reference chart together so that you can quickly look at all your options and choose the best technique in any given situation. (See Table 4.1 on the following page.)

TABLE 4.1 The Covert Persuasion Tactics
A Quick-Reference Summary Table

Rapidly build resonant rapport	Use content to build rapport	Use processes to build rapport	Synchronize with your target	Synchronize voices
Synchronize breathing	Synchronize posture and body movement	Testing synchronization	Alter the tone, pace and pitch of your voice	Induce reciprocity
Make the damaging admission	Share part of you with them	The common enemy	Short story about "them"	Give respect
Knock their socks off	Give more than you promised	Use understatement power	Be precise, then beat precision	Faster, easier, better
Be on the edge of your seat	Ask for compliance	Induce a sense of scarcity	Open the door to a friend	Associate the known/unknown
Feel part of the group	Create contrast	Don't ask why	Shift time reference	Unshakable credibility
Use space	Commitment and consistency	Covert hypnotic language patterns	Make body and words say the same thing	Outcome based thinking
Determine how they represent information	Feel, felt, found	Deletion, distortion, generalization	Note-taking	Lower your voice
80/20 rule and Covert Persuasion	Inoculation to persuade	Flexibility	Covertly empathetic mind	Artfully vague language
Power of three	Vocal stress in delivery	Experiential involvement	Persuading with attitude	Using music to persuade
Inconsistency	Fewer choices means more yeses	People believe what they say, not what you say	Be private in public	Oscillation at the decision point

5 | The Words of Covert Persuasion

There are certain words that have been proven to be much more persuasive than others. What follows is a list of the most persuasive words in the English language. Please refer to these pages often as you craft your advertisements, arguments, or conversations.

Word choice matters more than most people think. The 12 most persuasive words in English are:

You, Money, Save, Results, Health, Easy, Love, Discovery, Proven, New, Safety, Guarantee

In marketing you might want to add this dozen.

Free, Yes, Fast, Why, How, Secrets, Sale, Now, Power, Announcing, Benefits, Solution

Here is a comprehensive list for sales, marketing, dating, and all other communication:

Acclaimed, Advancement, Amazing, Announcing, Appealing, At Last, Attention, Authentic, Aware, Bargain, Because, Boosts, Breakthrough, Challenge, Change, Choice, Classic, Comfortable, Compare, Complete, Convenient, Delivers, Deserve, Discount, Discover, Discovery, Distinguished, Easy, Easily, Effective, Energy, Exceptional, Exciting, Exclusive, Experience, Experienced, Expert, Extraordinary, Fast, Free, Fresh, Fun, Guarantee, Heal, Help, Honest, How To, Hurry, Imagine, Important, Improved, Indispensable, Incredible, Informative, Instantly, Intimate, Introducing, Irresistible, Last Chance, Love, Luxurious, Magic, Miracle, Money, Money-making, Money-saving, Natural, Naturally, New, Now, Offer, Original, Overcome, Peace of Mind, Perfect, Please, Pleasure, Plus, Popular, Power, Powerfully, Practical, Prevents, Price Reduction, Profitable, Promise, Proven, Quickly, Realize, Recommended, Refreshing, Relax, Reliable, Relief, Relieve, Remarkable, Research, Results, Risk Free, Revolutionary, Romantic, Safety, Sale, Satisfaction, Save, Scientific, Secret, Security, Sensational, Service, Simplifies, Soothe, Special Offer, Status, Stop, Stimulating, Striking, Stylish, Superior, Surefire, Surprising, Thank You, Timely, The Truth About, Traditional, Trusted, Ultimate, Unlimited, Unusual, Useful, Valuable, Wanted, Warning, You, Yours.

$10,000 COVERT PERSUASION TRICK

Use the word "because" when answering anything asked of you, and you'll find people agreeing with you much more often. Use the word "because" when asking someone to comply with your request. People have an almost instant positive response to this word.

$10,000 COVERT PERSUASION TRICK

Compliance is gained more easily when you are asking a question that leads people where you want them to go. It's natural to want to tell the other person what to say, think, do, or feel. Unfortunately, if you do that, you'll meet with much more resistance. Instead, ask a question (or series of questions) that leads the other person to your conclusion. When done carefully, the other person feels that his opinion matters and that he has some control over a situation. In reality, of course, you are structuring his thought direction and range of responses.

How will you use some of these words today to get more of what you want, more often? Letters? Brochures? Verbal Communication? A few examples might help to show exactly how you may combine these words to get your point across:

"This scientifically *proven* program includes three *easy*-to-use techniques that will *change* your life forever."

"Would *you* like to *save money*?"

"How would *you* like to discover the secrets of this *new proven* technology?"

Use the words and form questions for greater impact. A lot of power is packed into a question. If you can get yourself to ask instead of tell, you will find success in stirring the internal motivations in the other person. You'll get him to want to help you.

$10,000 COVERT PERSUASION TRICK

To be a successful persuader, you must approach the process backwards. In other words, think of your goal (exactly what you want the outcome to be) and then design the questions that will lead your target to this goal. This sounds simple and straightforward, but it's not as easy as it sounds. Most people don't take the time to think this through in enough detail. It's hard work. It's what lawyers do when examining a witness in court. They plan their questions, word for word, to get the responses they want to impress the jury with the version of the case that best suits the lawyer. Depending on the im-

portance of your persuasion attempt, you may want to actually write out your questions word for word and anticipate possible responses. The more preparation you do, the more successful you will be.

Use Transformational Grammar

I listen carefully to the words people choose to describe their experiences in life. I've noticed that the words a person uses actually steer the feelings in the moment. In other words, if you say, "I feel totally devastated," you'll create different feelings in your mind and body than if you, in the very same situation, say "I'm curious. Why did things turn out this way?" The words you say become the feelings you feel. What you allow your mind to concentrate on is what you will create in your reality.

There's an entire category of psychological study that focuses on this one aspect. Noam Chomsky developed the theory in 1956 and labeled it "Transformational Grammar." The premise is simple. If you can change your words, you change your feelings and the mental state associated with them. You'll feel the power of words immediately. Change your words and you change how you feel inside too.

Transformational Vocabulary Self-Assessment Scenario

Read the following situation and then choose the multiple-choice answer that best fits your decision/reaction/response/action. You'll find out more about how you and your target think.

You're in an important company meeting and it's been announced that the company has made some mistakes, and the new line of Big Joe Action Figures is not selling. In fact, some small children have been injured, and their parents are suing the company. Times are tough. So, in an effort to save the company, 500 of the

4,000 employees are being laid off. You and your friends are among those 500. Your mind starts to race. What do you do?

A. You get *angry*. You've worked for the past five years for the company and have *given 100 percent*. This is how they pay you back? A layoff? Some *thanks*. What about *loyalty*? It isn't *fair*. There are some people who get to stay that are *lazy*. Why do *they* get to stay? You're *mad*.

B. You ask yourself why they included you in the group of 500 to be let go. You ask yourself, "What was it about me that *wasn't good enough?*"

C. You begin looking for a new job immediately. Secretly, you feel a sense of relief. You never really liked it at that company anyway. Now, you see this as a *blessing in disguise*. This is your *freedom*. The more you think about it, the more *excited* you become at all the *opportunity* you see in front of you.

D. Your friends all decide that this action is *grossly unfair*. They've talked to a lawyer and have decided to *sue*. They're putting together a class-action lawsuit. They've filed *grievances* with the local union. They're going to *demand* they get their jobs back. The more they talk, the more you feel they're right. You also think you have been *wronged*. You *deserve* to get your job back. You're right there with them.

Which one of the possible reactions is most like you—A, B, C, or D? Your choice will reveal a lot about the way you currently view the world.

A = Anger/Mad view of the world—a "*they owe me*" view

B = Questioning, but you tend to take it personally

C = "There are advantages to everything" outlook

D = Entitlement/Group must be treated fairly/democratic union mentality—"*they owe us*"

Realize, however, that ultimately you have a choice about how you react and what word labels you put on a given situation.

The bottom line is this: You must realize that the words you use to describe the experiences in your life to yourself and to others *become* the experiences. You choose your focus. You choose your attention's direction. You choose your words—you choose your feelings.

Commit yourself to using a mood-transforming vocabulary. Refer to the lists at the beginning of this chapter and begin to add as many of those words as possible to your daily, useable vocabulary.

6

The Focused Outcome Mindset

Covert persuasion, like anything else, works best when the desired outcome is predetermined.

Everything you want to have, be, or do begins in the mind. Your own mind is the starting point of all success. The object of your desire, whether it is a person, place, or thing is imagined in your mind, and only then can you formulate a plan to get it.

When you were a baby and you were hungry, you wanted to get the attention of your parents. So what did you do? You cried. It worked. You got the attention you needed, and you were fed. As basic as that sounds, it is pretty successful persuasion. This is a basic example of the concept of the Focused Outcome Mindset. The baby has a desire (fill this hunger pain), and the baby utilizes action (crying) in order to get what it wants (a satisfied tummy).

Formula: Desire → Focused Action(s) → Outcome

Persuasion begins in your mind. The clearer you are about exactly what you want, the better the chances of your actually getting it and being successful.

In my search to discover exactly what it is that separates the really successful people from the average performers, I've discovered one key trait. What is it that successful individuals do that separates them from the mediocre?

A Focused Outcome Mindset

There is a difference between the truly successful people and the ones who struggle. Do you want to know what it is? It's a *Focused Outcome Mindset*. Succeeding at anything takes discipline. Discipline means 100 percent effort, constant concentration, and a drive to succeed at your goal until the successful outcome is achieved. This drive is surprisingly lacking in the majority of people in all aspects of business today. For this reason, when you project a Focused Outcome Mindset and commit to building its power within you, you'll be many times more successful at achieving the outcomes you desire.

The Focused Outcome Mindset is the ability to imagine the goal or outcome in your mind, formulate the actions that need to be taken in order to achieve the outcome, and then take those actions until the goal is achieved.

Many benefits come from this concentrated mindset, not the least of which is the ability to convert every situation into an opportunity you can take advantage of.

Your ability to think at least one step ahead of your opponent is critical to your success. Who is your opponent? Your opponent is whoever or whatever stands between what you want and what you have right now.

One of the problems most people encounter is not knowing exactly what it is they want. They lack a focus. They allow themselves to be constantly distracted. They drift.

One of the toughest aspects of the Forced Focus Mindset is to maintain it. Everything attempts to distract you and divide your energy until you are aimlessly off on a tangent that doesn't advance you even one step toward your goal. In that moment you are not only lost, you are tired. You have wasted your efforts and your time. You will never get those minutes, hours, days, or months back.

To put a finer point on it, you're one day closer to your last day. Did you spend your day well? Did you invest your day wisely? Are you closer to your ultimate goal? If not, don't beat yourself up about it; refocus your mind and commit to starting over in the morning. Each day is a fresh start, and a chance to do what is good and right, and a chance to advance one step (or two or three steps) closer to your goal.

The Difference

Have you ever thought that some people are just lucky? Do you look at the captains of industry and think that everything just goes their way?

Stop it. Why do you think that way? It's wrong. Those people aren't lucky. They have worked very hard to achieve the success they're enjoying. The difference is focus. They have it, and they keep focused until they achieve. They have a clear picture of exactly what they want. In any given instant, the successful person will compare the object, situation, or person in front of him with his ultimate goal-focus. If the person, object, or situation will advance the successful person even one step toward his own goal focus, then he will make every effort to persuade the people involved to let him help advance them toward their own goal. If it does not, they will not allow themselves to spend time on an activity or with a person that does not advance his goal-focus.

Smashing That Idea Called Luck

Do you think that Bill Gates just seemed to stumble day after day onto good fortune and that over many days of good luck he was able to build a huge company and become the world's richest man? No! Bill Gates was not lucky. He had a vision, a focus, and a very clear set of goals that he was committed to achieve. He did not build Microsoft by accident or luck.

People with a Focused Mindset Are Easy to Spot

You'll notice people who are focused and clear regarding specific parts of their life. For example, people who have a health focus take action regarding their food and exercise habits. People with this focus will not get fat and out of shape. They will not let anything stand in the way of their workout. They won't allow it to be interrupted, sidetracked, or skipped. They are focused. They want the result, and they know the only way to guarantee that they will get it is to make sure they do the daily things necessary to be fit and healthy.

The sales professional with this mindset firmly rooted in mind will be strikingly more successful than all the others. It's actually easy to win more sales, make higher commissions, and build your client base when you adopt and perfect this mindset within yourself. However, whether you're in sales or not, a Focused Outcome Mindset is critical to persuading coworkers, bosses, customers, and prospects.

A Focused Mindset Gives You Immediate Confidence

Once you adopt this mindset and it becomes a habitually patterned way of thinking, you will begin to feel and exude a strong confidence that will attract the things, people, and situations that will help you succeed.

When you are in control of your own life, when you have a Focused Outcome Mindset, you will have the internal confidence to know what action to take (or not to take) next. It will almost seem as if you intuitively know how to persuade others more successfully than ever before. Believe it or not, a lot of people around you will begin to call you "lucky." Now, we've already destroyed that statement. There is no denying that this mindset requires a lot of work. And, of course, there is no "luck" involved. It's all about knowing with crystal clarity exactly what you want from every situation, every person, and every opportunity. Once you know that, you prepare yourself. Then when your preparation and focus meet the right opportunity, you have the best chance for success.

Why a "Focused" Outcome?

Without constant attention to your own thought processes, your brain will begin to go off track. It will become negative and open to the negative influences of the mass of struggling others. You must force your mind to focus on your ultimate outcome constantly and forever.

If you let your guard down, junk will get in. You must be vigilant. Other people are out to get you, or at least get your attention. They want your help on *their* priorities and goals. You can only afford to comply with their requests if in doing so it advances you toward your own.

This entire line of thinking may sound a little Machiavellian, and I suppose it is. But it is a slightly softer approach than that because it recognizes the need for other people and is aimed at the ultimate benefit of the greater good.

Focus Requires Energy

In order to focus on something, you have to have an energy, desire, or drive that is the fuel to propel your force. That energy comes in three root forms:

- *Food.* Eating in a healthy way and avoiding food with no nutritional value.

- *Mood.* Food is chemistry and it affects your blood and brain chemistry and significantly alters your mood and attitude. Being around others who share your ethics, values, and goals will keep your mood and attitude focused.

- *Sleep.* You must get enough sleep; your brain works while you sleep, and it needs this time so that it can function at its best during waking hours.

Success Is a Self-Project

Success is the result of your single-minded focus on what you want. The energy to sustain your drive must, and can, only come from within your own head. No one else will do it for you. The energy it takes is beyond all expectations. It takes far more than anyone thinks. That's why so few people are successful. It's lonely until the first success. Then, using the energy from that success, you fuel more successes.

Anticipating Three Steps Ahead

Many people struggle because they do not anticipate the actions of the important people around them. So, they find themselves in a re-active mode, rather than in a proactive mode. There is no power in being in reaction. In fact, all it does is drain your energy, and it usually benefits the other person (if anyone at all). If you find yourself in reaction, chances are very good that you are working on someone else's agenda and yours is neglected.

There is power in being proactive. You can anticipate and profit from the future actions of others if you allow yourself to spend a few minutes thinking sharply about the future. I'm not talking about the distant future, no, just about three steps ahead of where you and the people around you are right now. That will be sufficient to allow you to persuade (ethically, of course) the people around you to produce the outcome you want.

This takes a high level of energy, because with every passing minute, the three future steps will change. You must keep up. Don't underestimate the skill this takes.

Think about TV shows or chess moves. The characters in TV shows like *Survivor* plot against each other and try to predict the way the other people will act and who they will vote off the island. This prediction is a very tough mental action.

Anticipation is a habit pattern of thinking and acting that takes a commitment to persistence. It's easy to get lazy and fall behind.

Lazy Is the Natural State of Mind

If you don't anticipate, you'll be caught off guard and surprised, and that won't always be good. Unfortunately, without your commitment to pay constant attention to the anticipated actions and reactions of others, you'll fail. This will happen because the brain is a minimalist machine. Our brains like shortcuts and time-saving moves. We actually like to *avoid thinking* at all costs. If our brains see a way to avoid this tough task, they will choose that easy way—unless you are aware of this fault and take control.

I call this phenomenon *Mental Drift*. It's not that we don't want to pay attention; it's just that it's so easy not to. One failure to anticipate here, another one there, and in a flash we're behind. We're in reaction, out of control. All it takes to succeed is to *anticipate*. And to succeed at constantly anticipating, you must focus on it.

Because of Mental Drift, you must continue to focus. Otherwise your brain will choose the lazy road, the road of failure. Unfortunately, this is just the way our brains are wired. Knowing this happens allows you to be aware of it and to take action to prevent your mind from drifting.

The Urgent and Important Matrix

The Urgent and Important Matrix is a time management tool that incorporates the Focused Outcome Mindset and the power of covert persuasion (see Figure 6.1).

Make a prioritized list of actions based on where each person, event, or item in your life falls. Decide each item's importance based on your focus. That's a key point. If you stop and ask yourself where that particular item falls, determining its urgency and importance relative to your goal/focus, you will immediately place yourself in a more powerful position.

Quadrant I	Quadrant II
Urgent Not Important	**Urgent** Important
Quadrant III	Quadrant IV
Not Urgent Not Important	**Not Urgent** Important

FIGURE 6.1 Urgent and Important Matrix.

This evaluation takes place with well-formed questions. We'll discuss the power of questions later in this book. But know now that any time you are deciding what's important (and urgent) to you, you are asking yourself questions. Usually these are silent, and sometimes you don't even consciously know you are asking questions of yourself, but you are. You constantly talk to yourself.

It's been said that you should be careful what you ask for because you'll get an answer. That's true. Your brain is very efficient. Whatever you ask it, it will provide you an answer. It doesn't matter if it's good or bad, positive or negative, it will answer. So, be very careful.

Back to the matrix. The key to using it effectively is to know that there is a point before someone else's priority gets onto your to-do list, a point at which you get to decide. You get to ask yourself, "How urgent and how important is this?" The most important thing here is to know that you get to decide. There is no rule that says that just because something is urgent and important for someone else that it should be that way for you. It doesn't work that way unless, due to mental drift, you let it.

From this point forward, you must be aware that you make all the decisions for you. You decide what the priority of each item, person, or event is in your day. Other people may suggest, but they can't place it in your matrix, only you can do that.

Focused Outcome is a concept that stems from the ability to take responsibility for your own life. Upon realizing that you are in total control of your own thoughts; you can direct them, channel them, and focus them onto the path that will get you the result you are after.

One of the forces in life that will try to sidetrack you is what I call the "victim virus." I have written about this in the past, and I believe that all of us at one point or another have become infected. Whether it's a temporary infection or something that turns chronic is entirely up to you.

First, let's explore this "victim virus" and then we'll tie it into the Focused Outcome concept.

The Victim Virus

Do you think life is unfair? Do you feel singled out? Do you think other people are out to get you? Are other people making you feel inferior, dumb, stupid, or confused? Do you find it easy to blame someone or something for the way things turn out, low sales, lost promotions, lack of cooperation with your coworkers?

If you answered yes to any of these questions, you may be a victim. But don't worry, there's something you can do to transform yourself from victim to successful covert persuader.

Do You Have the Victim Virus (VV)?

Blame is a virus. Once you blame someone else for an outcome you don't like, you have become infected. It's an extremely powerful, quick spreading, and devastating virus. The news gets worse. There is no drug you can take to rid yourself of this virus. Oh, come on, is it really that bad? Yes.

I'm sure you've noticed there are vast differences in people. Some are very successful and some are poor. Some have even given up on life. How sad. The answer lies in this Victim Virus.

The unsuccessful, poor, and beaten-down people all around us are infected. They have full-blown cases of the Victim Virus. You'll hear the victims *blame* the economy, their parents, their boss;—the list is usually endless. Beware! Because they are infected with a virus, they are highly contagious. It doesn't take long for them to infect others and build a support group of victims.

Most people will be polite and agree with the blamer. Most

people will see that it's obviously the other person's fault. They'll agree that the victim is right and that the other person should be blamed for the outcome. It's easy. It's nonconfrontational. It's simple.

Why Do People Blame?

People blame because they refuse responsibility. Sometimes that is not clear to the person doing the blaming. Sometimes the victim has followed this blaming pattern since he was young and doesn't see any other options. Why am I calling these blamers "victims"?

The definition of a "victim" (blamer) is:

A person who feels tricked, swindled, or taken advantage of— that he has no power, is controlled by others, and believes others are to blame for his situation.

Victims feel out of control of their own lives. They are convinced that other people have power and control over them. It's an illusion, but it's all they see. They believe this is the reality. They feel at the mercy of others (sometimes only a few specific others).

Terminally Infected Brain

Victims are suffering from a devastating, destructive, and terminally infected brain. They have a brain that is full of Victim Virus, made up of thousands of strains of powerful viruses that no pill or liquid will eliminate.

Is there a cure? Yes. But, ironically, victims don't believe there is one. They believe other people have caused their circumstances, and they believe that a solution, if there is one, can only be found in some other person. They look to another person to provide the cure for their miserable lives. When the other person fails to make things better, the victim blames him. The problem here is an habitual failure to look inside his or her own mind. No other person has any power to cure. The cure is within.

How Do These People Change?

Many do not. Some do, but it takes the world, or a very special individual, to shock them, to interrupt their dependency pattern. After this shock, the internal process begins. They must begin the journey of "self-improvement." This overused phrase makes it sound easy. It makes it sound like you can go to the bookstore and find one of a thousand books under the "Self-Help" section, read it, and everything will be better. Nothing could be further from the truth.

The fallacy in believing that a book will change your life is a victim trap. If you believe this, then you are following the victim's path. You are looking to someone or something outside of yourself to fix the situation. And if it doesn't work, you also have someone or something to blame. It's a wicked, never-ending circle of self-deception.

On the other hand, you can improve your life with the *help* of books. They can help you to change your life. The change comes from you, not from the book. You are the key to your success, and books, seminars, and other people are all tools available to you to make the life you want. The victim trap is in believing that the book will fix the problem. The way of success is knowing that the change for the better has to come from inside your own head, but the book can provide you with some raw material (information, techniques, tips, etc.) to help you make the change happen. The difference is in the focus. Victims are externally focused. Successful people are internally focused. They have forced their focus onto exactly what they want. They have committed themselves to learning more and better ways to persuade others to help them get more of what they want more often. They have an unshakable goal that they focus on all the time. That is what separates the truly successful salesperson from the average performers.

Dependency?

Yes, victims are dependent on others for approval, decisions, and acceptance. They react to others. But what does it really mean to be dependent?

Being dependent is a sad state of life. Look at this definition: "*the state of being determined, influenced, or controlled by something else.*" I would change this slightly for our purposes to read: "*the state of being determined (decided on), influenced, and controlled by someone else.*"

I'll admit that, to a certain extent, everyone is dependent on everyone else. Otherwise our economy, our world, would not work. But that is not what I am talking about. In the personal lives of victims, the word "dependent" takes on a significant and most likely destructive meaning.

A change in direction of thought and action must take place. Everything begins on the inside and then flows to the world outside your mind and brain. Previous to this revelation, it all flowed in the opposite direction. It used to be that other people made decisions, and it all flowed into the victim's brain, and that's the way life is. Wrong. Reverse it. Take control. Begin to see that you have a brain that is totally capable of making good, strong, and right decisions. Realize that you are in control of your life and that decisions flow from you, not to you.

Victims Need to Change the Word

Vocabulary is the first giant step. Simply eliminating the word "victim" is a start. You can no longer call yourself a victim once you realize you have complete control of your own life. You must use a different word.

Words are powerful. Words are the key to massive personal change. There is an entire field of study called Transformational Grammar/Transformational Vocabulary. The entire basis of this field of study is the fact that words label our experience. If you do not use the word, you cannot feel the feeling. And of course, the opposite is true—if you use the word, you feel the feeling.

As an example, I might ask you about your workload at your job and you answer, "It's overwhelming!" Well then, you will feel overwhelmed. But if instead you say, "It's exciting!", then you will have a totally different physiological response. You will feel energized. The work amount is exactly the same, but the way you choose to label the experience with words makes all the difference in how you feel.

You choose how you feel. Other people don't have the power to make you feel anything unless you give them that power. Choose your words carefully. They matter.

Salespeople as Victims?

Absolutely yes. It's hard to believe that people who make their living by convincing others of the rightness of the decision to buy would be some of the biggest victims. But it's true.

$10,000 Covert Persuasion Trick
The 80/20 Rule. In this case, it means that 80 percent of salespeople are often suffering from the Victim Virus. The upper 20 percent of salespeople do not suffer this thinking virus and therefore are very successful. I want to concentrate on the 80 percent, many of whom can be helped by simply realizing that what they are doing is the reason they are not successful.

Why? Salespeople are an odd bunch. As we look closely at that 80 percent, we'll discover some interesting things. They like to blame, and they've become good at it. It provides them with an inoculation against responsibility because they infuse their blame and victim thinking with belief. In other words, the longer they engage in this thinking, the more they tend to believe it. This method of thinking is fatal to success, but they can't see it.

Sales Management is Unfair

This is just one of the thousands of accusations that are thrown at the management of the typical sales force. Why does the victim say or think this? Because he is not successful. Victims blame their lack of sales on the management's demand for reports or call sheets or some other form of activity tracking that the salesperson thinks is unnecessary, demeaning, or stemming from a root of mistrust. The top 20 percent of salespeople do their reports and get on with selling. They may not like them, but they do them and move on. The bottom 80 percent do not. They see this intrusion as a chance to blame management for their low sales.

It's interesting that the 80 percent complainers and blamers never look at the top 20 percent and find out what they're doing. Those top 20 percent are the ones that are accepting full and complete responsibility for their decisions and actions. They're not blaming or playing the victim. They've either never had the Victim Virus or they have cured themselves of it.

Objections

The economy is slow, people aren't buying, their budget is spent, they use the other guys . . . and on and on. The victim salesperson will accept and readily believe these objections. They are almost relieved that they can blame their lack of sales on the economy or some other scapegoat. This allows them to escape personal responsibility for their lack of sales. They view themselves as the victim of the economy or whatever the objection was—it's not their fault. They can blame someone or something else. They feel justified in the case they present to their management. They believe strongly that they are totally in the right and that forces beyond their control have conspired to reduce the amount of product or service that it is possible to sell. Notice that I didn't say these various forces *have* conspired to reduce the amount of product that was possible for them to sell. No, I said the amount that was possible to be sold. The difference is that in stating it this way, the salesperson has removed himself from the equation. This is significant, because he cannot be held responsible. This is what the victim wants—freedom from responsibility. Victims want others to realize that the reasons for their low sales are beyond their control.

I Don't Blame the Customer, It's This Company

Many victim-thinking salespeople blame their lack of results on the "ridiculous requirements" of the company they work for. They believe the management is completely out of touch with the real selling activity. They view the requirements for call sheets and call planners and tallies of calls as a time-consuming and even a time-wasting exercise. They further believe that this exercise is designed only to cover the ass of the sales manager who needs to prove to senior management that progress is being made. They feel very adversarial about the role of the company and how it negatively impacts their ability to make sales. They feel they are the victims of an out-of-touch, report-happy company that doesn't know what it's really doing. They feel they are the victim.

In Conclusion

Does any of this sound familiar? You may have recognized a little bit of the Victim Virus in you. That's okay. If you realize it, chances are very good that you now realize that you have the power to take complete control of and responsibility for your life. That control can improve your life, if you take responsibility and action. That's the only way to cure yourself of the Victim Virus.

You may have also noticed these traits in other people you know in all types of settings like work, home, and social events. As you read the above paragraphs, you may have thought of someone you know who is currently playing his role in life as a victim. If you did, you have a choice. You can be the shocker for this person. Jolt him. Make him realize what's going on and give him the opportunity to take control of his own life back again. Or, you can be an enabler. But be careful. If you choose this route, chances are good you'll eventually be infected.

Utilize the Focused Outcome Mindset

The bottom line is, take complete control of *your* life. Realize that you are responsible for every decision you make, and that only you can choose how you feel, what you do, and what the outcome really means to you. Realize that only you can cure yourself of the Victim Virus, and you can do it by a decision, a *Focused Outcome Mindset!*

The "Victim Virus" translates directly into the Focused Outcome Mindset concept. Simply put, if you allow your mind to become weak enough, you'll become infected with VV and will not be able to proactively focus your efforts in a way that moves you forward. Instead, you will be distracted, dejected, and demotivated. You will fail, or at the very least, you will become a member of the struggling many instead of the successful few. You'll find persuasion to be very difficult, and you'll be right.

However, the truth is, it's actually easier to persuade and win. When you put the Covert Persuasion techniques to work in your sales career, you'll notice a huge increase in your ability to more successfully, covertly persuade your boss, coworkers, customers, and even friends and family. It's all because you'll be persuading others with your 100 percent congruent message and they will feel compelled to comply.

7

20 Keys to Using Covert Persuasion in a Story

The Intention of Communication Is to Influence

In this chapter I'm going to show you how to influence with story. First I'm going to reveal the 20 Keys to Using Covert Persuasion in Story and then I'm going to show you exactly how you might present information in story form to an audience or another person.

Most communication does not succeed in achieving the intended result. Why? Because most communication is not created or delivered with intention.

Covert Persuasion (Intentional Subtle Influence) is often best used in a story, and in fact it makes the story far more likely to succeed in achieving the intended result, influencing others to your way of thinking. Think about what happens when most people tell a story, particularly in a group. The story is boring. It's about how the car in front of them cut them off. They nearly died. People can't wait to escape.

For an example, read the following story.

The room was packed with people. We were all sitting down to

142

eat, 22 of us at one big long table. We were on our lunch break from training. I was sitting next to Ron Stubbs (co-trainer in this event), who was talking with our friend Katherin. I was sitting opposite a woman whose face was a blur and whose name escapes me, but the moment was memorable for me.

The waitress had been gone for almost 20 minutes before lunch was served. The woman across from me had been talking for the entire time. My head was nodding because I wanted to be affable. I was tired, but she never noticed that I didn't hear a word after the first five or six minutes.

I do remember she told me all about her trip to Sedona. There was something said about an energy vortex. Any time I hear "energy vortex" or anything like that some of me is ready for engagement. But I was tired, and soon her stories drifted from the energy vortex to a trip she had just taken and then . . . I don't remember . . . anything. I was sipping a diet drink with lemon and nodding. I heard Ron and Katherin talking about the training, and I heard the hum of ten other voices in the room chatting away.

Ron whispered in my ear, "Hey buddy, you in a trance or what?" (I know he said this because he told me later that he did.) Apparently I blinked my eyes. The woman across from me said, "Don't you think?"

It dawned on me she had been telling me a story for what seemed like forever, and I had simply drifted off into the ether. Fortunately, only Ron noticed.

He laughed into my ear. I immediately felt uncomfortable, but I managed to say "I can see that." (It is an automatic response I've learned that gets you out of trouble when you don't understand, can't hear, or have spaced out from abject boredom.)

Ron put his left arm around my back grabbing my left shoulder. His right hand grabbed my right shoulder. He looked at the woman across the table.

"I need him for two minutes and then you can have him back."

Ron whispered in my ear, "I just saved you psychiatric help . . . you owe me big." And I did. He actually saved the entire class because the woman's stories had shut me down and sent me past Neptune. Ron talked a little about what he wanted to go over that day and then, mercifully, lunch arrived.

Captivate Your Listener

A story about boredom—and it can be captivating! Stories can captivate to the point where you are experiencing everything as if you were there with the storyteller. A story can also completely shut down the listener. It takes very little time to drive someone past boredom and drop them off at exhaustion junction.

When you are telling a story, it should have a purpose. Answer the following three questions and note the tips in numbers 4 through 20.

#1 What intention do you have?

Why are you telling this story? What is the point? What is the purpose? Are you telling it for fun, to make people laugh? Or is there no point whatsoever—are you just talking without thinking?!

#2 What do you want the other person to think or feel after you tell your story?

Don't think, "Maybe they will like me." Do think, "I want them to know that I care and that their problem is something I'm interested in."

Or, do think, "I want them to feel better, so I won't tell a story that's worse than the one they told. I will listen for a while before even thinking of telling a story."

Sometimes it's best to not tell any story. That is something the most powerful storytellers practice.

#3 What is your purpose?

I don't mean the intention of this specific story, but the point of your being wherever it is you are with this person or group and then thinking, what is my plan? What stories will help me persuade them that I'm credible, interested, concerned, and want them to come out on top too? What brief story or stories do I have in my repertoire that help illustrate what I want to happen here?

You say to yourself, "I am telling this story to Kevin because I want him to_____," and you make sure your story moves Kevin in that direction.

If people thought in advance why they were telling a story, they would tell far fewer stories. My intention of telling you a story must be clear to me or I don't tell it.

COVERT PERSUASION FACT

Stories can kill rapport or captivate to a plane far above rapport to a place of connection that is almost electric.

Note: Just because you intend to tell a story for a specific result doesn't mean you will get that specific result. It often will be filtered through people's beliefs, biases, and values, and the story could be offensive or felt in a negative way. That will happen particularly when you tell a story to more than one person.

Know two things: First, It's not the intention of every story you or I tell to deliver a calm message. Many messages must ignite emotions to influence people. The other notion is that if you get similar feedback from multiple people you might want to reconsider the value or usefulness of a specific story.

Keep this caveat in mind: The best communicators are often those who generate the most emotion, positive and negative, in others. When you remember Bill Clinton or Ronald Reagan, you recall two very different people and sets of beliefs, also two successful communicators that were generally respected by the majority of people, even those who disagreed with them. Emotion influences.

Key Point: Capture, hold and focus the audience's attention until they go into a natural waking trance. Share information in a simplistic fashion that appeals to the audience's innate curiosity and need to learn.

#4 Give powerful singular self-revelations that reveal and teach the audience your values, beliefs, the goodness of your heart, and the emotional and experiential reasons for it.

That said; put all the emphasis on *singular*. If you tell a story that is a biography or a travelogue of your entire life trip, the other person completely loses interest.

If you want someone to know that you value loyalty or you believe in God or you are a Red Sox fan, you must stick to the singular. Pick one covert message and stick with that message.

Avoid communicating too much, and avoid too much information in any one story. A good story maxes out at about four minutes in conversation with one person. You can tell one of those about every half hour. With small groups you have to make your stories tighter and more concise. With large groups of 50 or more, you can tell a longer story (perhaps six or seven minutes.) if it is emotional or action-packed.

You want to self-reveal because you must get the person you are communicating with to empathize with you, to know who you are inside. But self-reveal in a nonthreatening fashion.

Always put words of self-flattery back into the mouths of the people who originally said the words. If you want to convey how smart you are, make sure your story is one where someone else tells you how smart you are. This is the beauty of "covert." It's why a testimonial means so much more to the average person than a scientific study. A testimonial that is singular in its message is always more effective than a testimonial that says you are smart, good looking, and a good gardener.

A good story must:

1. Have a clear purpose or intent, a particular influence you wish to achieve by telling it.

2. Have intention. You must be clear in your own mind, "I am telling this story in order to get my listeners to _____!"

People babble and babble and say nothing, have no clue what their intention is, and worse, have no idea that the other person can't hear them any more because his mind is just west of Neptune. You always have a clear intention and pay very close attention to feedback, verbal and nonverbal, from your listener.

#5 Capture, hold, and focus the audience's attention until they enter into a state of captivation.

A "state of captivation" is accurate. When a person is completely wrapped up in what you are saying and there is nothing else happening in the world, you have a *state of captivation*. You have created a tunnel between you and your listener, and you are meeting in the tunnel. You will meet the other person at his end and take him by the hand and bring him to your side.

What grabs attention?

- Something they passionately agree with you about (pro-life/pro-choice, handgun/ban handgun, and so forth).

- Something controversial that creates an attention-getting emotion inside of them (anything that causes emotion that is not so great as to take attention away from your story or nor so dull that they pay no attention).

- Peripheral things that have nothing to do with the actual content of the story (camera focuses on the cheerleaders between plays to hold attention in commercial breaks).

- Setting, environment. Where the story is told (the restaurant you are in), or if you are good, where the story takes place in the mind of the person you are talking to.

Self-Evaluation:

What grabs my attention about your product or service?

_____

_____

There's more than this, but this is the key: You want to wake up your listeners. Get them OUT of their walking-through-life trance, and then bring them into your world. You want to stimulate an emotion, but not to a degree that they become compelled to argue with you or debate you about something. You stir emotion; you don't boil it. Stir and you captivate. Boil and you eliminate.

I was in the 14th row at the MGM Grand Garden Arena in Las Vegas. Paul McCartney was on tour promoting his new album. I heard these lyrics, "There's a fine line between courage and recklessness . . . a fine line between chaos and creation." They're simple lyrics yet profound, and one of the reasons that he is such an ingenious storyteller through song.

McCartney 2005. That's the deal. Your story is told because the listeners are fascinated and don't want to walk away. They are not repelled. They are magnetized with interest. There can be tension. It must be relieved at times during the story.

A scary story works as long as listeners feel no compulsion to run. It makes their hearts beat faster but not to the point of a panic attack. You tell some detail, but make sure you keep unnecessary detail out. Detail can become very boring, very quickly. In seconds you can lose captivation and even simple attention. Rapid digression can then recapture a drifting mind if you put the mind back into the story at a quick pace. Lots of things captivate, but it's important that each sentence ends with certainty that your listener is fascinated.

#6 Share information in a simplistic fashion that appeals to the listener's innate curiosity and need to learn and acquire knowledge.

Never try to be too smart or too stupid for your listeners. Bring everything to their level of comprehension, and do not make a mistake by going too high or too low. If I'm not in the military, don't tell me you are going to the PX to get some food. Meet the listener on his landscape.

People want to know things, particularly secrets. They want to understand the way things work if it's easy to understand. Otherwise you can forget it and move on. Keep your story simple and emotion-filled if the subject of your story is not technical things.

#7 Reveal that you are humble.

People want to know you and trust you, to believe in you. Tell a story in your most humble voice that reveals who you really are to the listener. Arrogance is explosive and never good. It breaks rapport and causes decaptivation and attention deficit.

#8 Create vivid visualizations by giving descriptors that appeal to both the senses and the emotions.

Trigger as many safe or relatively safe places in the brain as you can. Communicate what you see, hear, feel, and smell. Cause the other person to almost hallucinate those sensations as well. That's captivation.

#9 Regress and/or progress the audience through time, deliberately avoiding the present as you do so.

Get the audience out of today back to some other time. The present is where they feel uncomfortable. Once in the future or past you can take them somewhere that you have discovered to be helpful in meeting the needs of captivation.

Get them in the moment. Never talk about your biography. Tell a story, a single story, and never tell another without demand until they have told one as well.

#10 Be real, be true, and be your own experience.

The story won't be the same every time because it won't be scripted. But the heart, the soul will be awesome. No matter the situation, beware of telling a story without thinking about why you are telling each part. You need to have intention and purpose. And it must align in some parallel way with your listener.

#11 It must somehow provide historically verifiable convincers of the reality, e.g. names, dates, places, that appeals to the audience's collective experience or memory.

This is one of the most powerful covert techniques in the book. Develop a recollection for dates and locations. Remember where the things you experienced took place. These details weave a web of credibility and thus reduce resistance dramatically.

People want to have what they consider evidence that something is true. Names, dates, and places don't prove anything, but they, at minimum, create an illusion in the listener's mind that the story is true. And truth matters. When people hear names, places, things, dates, they can be there with you, and when they are there, you are telling the truth because they can see, hear and feel it too.

The story can be fiction or fact, but if listeners hear names, dates, places, times, it is not fiction; it becomes part of memory. It becomes part of their understanding of truth and who you are. And when people know who you are, they like you more, and they like you instantly.

#12 When you are telling a story that involves other people, have the characters come alive by speaking directly in the first person, rather than indirectly in the third.

No one does this anymore and yet it is powerful. "He said, 'I'm doing the best I can, man,'" vs. "He said that he was doing the best he could!"

As you make a character real, it gives life to your story. I can't tell you how many people tell me they remember the story about the little girl in the wheelchair I met in Chicago during my first book tour. There are others that people tell me they remember, but they all remember Barnes and Noble, Chicago, July 1996.

#13 Your story must contain important embedded intentions, lessons, or keys to achieving your or someone else's purpose.

Example: I'm telling a story to a woman that Al really wants to take on a date. I'd like her to attend *Influence: Boot Camp* in February. (*Influence: Boot Camp* is my live signature event I hold in Las Vegas every year.) Two separate intentions that can both be met to create a triple win.

". . . and by the way, Al wasn't the only one who went to *Influence: Boot Camp* last year that got a book deal utilizing information he learned."

She knows that Al went to *Boot Camp*, and that he got a book deal, and that the information he got at *Boot Camp* was stuff he could actually use. Multiple purposes can be sandwiched into a story about Al with ease. One sentence, then I can return to telling a story about Al and how amazing he was when he presented at *Boot Camp*.

#14 You must place yourself in a context and situation that makes you relatable to the audience.

This is accomplished by either direct or visualized common experience. The audience must be able to say, "Yeah, that was just like when I . . ." Or, if they have no similar reference, you must at least appeal to the sense of curiosity, "Yeah, I've always wondered what it would be like to . . ." Yes. I'm just like the listener.

"Who'd have ever thought it . . . there I am . . . Kevin Hogan, a kid from Chicago, wondering if my tie looks good. . . . wondering if it's obvious that my heart is pounding away, seated across the table from one of the most important people in Poland."

It's easy to relate to someone being nervous, and we all like to be with someone important so remarks like those above make the story that I'm about tell completely relatable, something a listener can connect with easily and instantly.

#15 Sometimes you want to have meaning.

Your story can contain points of information that could have been told directly but are instead woven in as part of the tale. The lesson is usually learned by me (the storyteller) from someone else in the story. That way I'm not preaching. I'm learning and relating what I learned, as it happens, in the past. "I never realized how important it was to X."

And that is my message for the listener or audience. I want them to X, but I'm not telling them to X. I'm simply telling them that I previously had never realized how important it was to X.

#16 Very graciously tell your listener or audience how great and real you are. But you don't tell your listener, the people in your story do.

". . . and Kevin, we got a letter from the management of that Barnes and Noble. They said it was the best experience they ever had with an author." You can't tell your listener how wonderful you are, but the people in your story can . . .

#17 Charismatic covert charm and irresistible attraction is achieved by putting words of praise on the lips of other people in the story.

You can also offset what might be seen as boasting with self-deprecating humor or humility. And of course always reveal your vulnerabilities, inadequacies, weaknesses and plain ordinary "human-ness." Every great story I tell includes a great deal of self-deprecation— lots of vulnerability, plenty of personal exposure and human weakness. That's what my audience wants, and that's what they connect with. Self-deprecation is the trademark of great story.

#18 Give the listener opportunity to believe, have faith, and create her own trance-identified solutions in your story.

You want her to think, "Well, if she did that, then I can . . ." Put another way, if you can get listeners to say x instead of telling them x, they will more readily acquiesce and with more power and attitude.

#19 Provide clear inspiration, a nudge, to a specific action.

Your story should be simple, powerful, and memorable enough that listeners will repeat it, both mentally and verbally, and fully reexperience it when they do. All the classic stories in the repertoire can be told to someone else that they meet on the street, and it's always followed by, "Oh my gosh, he's such a great guy or, such a great speaker . . . you know what he said?"

Notice the power of being "in the moment."

#20 Use quotes.

Compare and contrast these examples carefully.

He looked at me like I was nuts. "Kevin, you idiot. What are you doing? Have you lost your mind?"

vs.

He looked at me like I was nuts and called me an idiot.

She locked eyes with mine and said, "Kevin Hogan, I love you."

vs.

She locked eyes with mine and told me she loved me.

He looked at me, shocked. "Kevin, you did that? It's amazing! You are incredible. How did you do it?!"

vs.

He looked at me shocked. He told me I was amazing and wanted to know how I did it.

It's this simple . . . or this hard. Now, here is the next big disaster or disaster averted.

> Key Bonus Point: You are telling a story. Not a biography. One story.

Stories are almost always events. One day, or one hour, or two similar related events, one causing the other. If you tell two stories before your listener has told one, you are at the cliff's edge. It's time to be quiet. Remember, in covert hypnosis, the key is subtle. The most common problems in story are bragging, boasting, and boring.

Those boastful words must come from someone else's mouth, or they don't get said. Compare these two statements:

Option 1: "Kevin: I'm such a great speaker and writer and renaissance man."

vs.

Option 2: Someone else saying, "Kevin you are just an amazing speaker and a brilliant writer! How did you become a renaissance man?" I shrink away not knowing what renaissance really is. I think that's a good thing but I don't know.

Notice how in Option 2, you covertly tell the world all this neat stuff because your fan said it to you. No one can argue or react negatively to the fan. But, they can think you are conceited if you say it yourself.

Now you've learned the 20 Keys of Telling a Story with Covert Persuasion. Let's take a story or two and show you just how to use these tools. Imagine that I'm on stage, telling the following story to an audience. There will be no quotes because everything you will read is what I say with the exception of what is in brackets. That's the analysis for you to see what is happening covertly!

The story starts like this:

Each of us sells something if we are to be successful in life. We all exchange our time and energy for dollars. The more assertive and successful we are, the better we are paid. And so does everyone else, because every person on earth owes an eternal debt of gratitude to people because without people there would be no jobs for anyone.

[I just told my audience of salespeople that they deserve a debt of gratitude and they are the people who create jobs. This is true. They know it, and I know it, and I recognize it without being patronizing.]

I discovered this early in my life. It was the autumn of 1972, and I realized that selling was my only hope.

[The immediate transition of letting each audience member know precisely how important they are is ideal for this . . . and then notice the date . . . 1972. Dates are credibility.]

I started selling when I was 10 years old. I had to. I was the oldest of five children and we had no money. My stepfather was going to die in less than 18 months, and mom's time was divided between her job and taking care of dad, who was confined to a hospital bed in our home. It was a heck of a way to live; we lived in a lower-middle-class suburb of Chicago. If I wanted to have money for anything, and I did, I would have to sell something.

I sold my services in the wintertime as the kid on the street who would shovel your driveway. $1 per hour. The Chicago winds would blow out of the north and off the lake with a bitter coldness that I'll never forget. Sometimes I'd take the $3 I would earn and give it to mom. Sometimes I'd keep the money and buy Pepsi and Reese's. In the summer, I would sell my services cutting people's lawns or pulling weeds. I hated pulling weeds.

Realizing that there was no hope for me in lawn and garden services, I knew at age 10 I would have to do something where I could utilize my time in a far more efficient manner. I saw an ad in a Sunday newspaper for Cheerful House Greeting Cards. I read that I could earn from fifty cents to two dollars for each box of cards sold. I immediately sent the company my $10 for a sample kit. ($10 was a lot of money in those days.) In return Cheerful House sent me five boxes of Christmas cards. Some quick math calculations revealed that if I just sold the five boxes I'd make one dollar per box sold! The sales literature said that there would only be four "selling seasons" per year, so whatever money was going to be earned would have to last a long time.

I got home from school the next day and as soon as my paper route was done I was ready to go make some real money. I knocked on my neighbor's door. It was Mrs. Gossard. I showed her my cards and she bought a box. My first dollar was earned! Then I went to Mrs. Singer. She couldn't buy a box. Mrs. Hendricks bought two boxes, Mrs. Serdar bought a box. Mrs. Makela bought a box. Lots of other people didn't. I was gone until 8:00 P.M. and had knocked on 30 doors and sold about 18 boxes of cards. I looked at my watch as the sun was setting. I knew I had to go home and help put the kids to bed. I had checks totaling about $60, of which my math whiz brain figured $20 was mine.

[Notice the specific names of the people in my neighborhood. They add credibility to the story and captivate the listener.]

Mom was so excited when she saw the order sheet. I told her that I'd give her all the money I earned. She said, "No. You earned it; you are going to keep it." Wow! The next day I left the neighborhood to start selling in a neighborhood I never went to. I was out from the time my paper route was done until sunset. I sold only four boxes of cards. Some of the people's houses were scary looking, and being a skinny little kid, I decided that I wouldn't go back there again. Nevertheless, I made about $4. I showed Mom when I got home, and she told me that it was mine to keep.

The problem was that I knocked on about 50 doors to earn that $4. I couldn't believe that more people didn't buy my Christmas cards. They obviously weren't as smart as the people in my neighborhood. The next day was Saturday, and I remember getting up, delivering the Saturday morning *Waukegan News Sun* (They had to be delivered by 7 A.M.) cutting the lawn, and then at noon off I went on my bicycle. I went into neighborhoods I had never been to and knocked on over 100 doors that day. I didn't stop to eat lunch or dinner. I sold 6 boxes of cards. I got home to find that there was no Hamburger Helper left. (I was eternally grateful.) I told Mom that I didn't have a very good day. I made $6, but I was driving across highways, and I was kind of scared of the neighborhoods I was going into. She suggested I stick with the neighborhoods where people knew me and that I wouldn't be crossing the highways anymore. (She would later tell me she was scared to death that her son was going into some of the neighborhoods.)

We totaled the order sheet. I had sold 28 boxes of cards. My total earnings would be about $30. I would get paid after I delivered all of the cards to my clients. I couldn't wait! I learned a lot that week. [I Kevin Hogan, have the capacity to learn. I don't know everything.] I learned that people were more likely to buy from me if they knew me. I realized that if people had the money, I could talk them into buying an extra box for someone else as a gift.

I learned that selling cards was a lot better than cutting the lawn, pulling weeds, shoveling snow, or delivering the newspaper. I learned I could work only four weeks per year selling cards. Selling cards was going to make me $100 per year, but I'd need to think of something else to sell if I was going to make more money.

More important, after delivering the cards to the people, I realized how much fun it was to see people smile and say "Thanks, Kevin." "They're beautiful." "You got those to me faster than I expected."

[Look at all the quotes! Look at what they say about my product and my personal service.]

Most important, I made $30 for about 20 hours of work that was not physically killing my scrawny 10-year old body! [See the self-deprecation. I'm weak. I'm a scrawny kid . . . and I was!]

I sold greeting cards for the next four years as a source of income. I sold flower seeds and vegetable seeds. (I also continued to sell my body shoveling snow, pulling weeds, cutting lawns, and doing anything I could.) The most fun was selling cards. The women were (for the most part) fun to talk with, the work was all sitting down in their living room and some of them even gave me cookies and milk those few days per year when I was selling. I was actually having fun working at something.

The ad from Cheerful House Greeting Cards changed my life. Not because it made me rich. It didn't. It gave me hope that I could escape living in poverty. The Boy Scouts wouldn't need to bring me clothes and turkey dinners on Thanksgiving anymore. (The Boy Scouts delivered clothing and food to our home on Thanksgiving on a couple of occasions. I remember appreciating the clothes and food and hating being needy.) I knew whatever I was going to do when I was older, it would be selling. I was right.

I discovered as a 10-year old that the ability to think quickly and talk with people could give me a chance to escape being poor and maybe—just maybe—be rich. Selling was hard work in some ways, but it was fun. It certainly beat "physical work!"

Selling would give me security, freedom, independence, and the ability to be productive, to be valuable to other people. It was something I could do well.

Fast forward to 1998. [Another date!]

It's autumn 1998. I've been earning a six-figure income for a few years. I've owned my own business, consulted or sold for other people since 1987. The idea of receiving an hourly wage and punching a time clock is almost a phobia. Business is good. I have several books in print including one, *The Psychology of Persuasion*, that is doing pretty well in the bookstores.

[Gently slide in the income; that is credibility in itself.]

But I've stalled. I've stagnated. I've been earning $1,000 to $2,000 per speech I give. Nothing wrong with that but I've been there and done that. What is going on? No one is offering me more than that. I am baffled. People compare my speaking style to Anthony Robbins and my physical and offstage presence to

Kelsey Grammar, David Letterman, and Drew Carey. Now, what more could a guy want? That's enough talent to feed off of for four lifetimes.

[Wouldn't most people be thrilled to have $1000 for an hour's work? Wouldn't most people want to be compared to David Letterman and Tony Robbins? Notice how it feels as you hear this.]

Then one day, I ran into Dottie Walters, the author of *Speak and Grow Rich*. Dottie owns the world's most prestigious speakers bureau and publishes *Sharing Ideas* magazine for national speakers.

I see her "Speak and Grow Rich" course listed next to mine in the Open U adult education catalog. I have no time to take a full day off and learn what I already know regardless of who is teaching it. But for years I have wanted to meet Dottie. She would now be about 70 or maybe older, and it was her book, *Speak and Grow Rich*, that helped me focus my world into teaching and speaking in public for a significant portion of my current living. I decided to take the Saturday off and go see Dottie. If nothing else, I should thank her for being inspirational in my life.

I experienced her class with about 20 other students. I enjoyed watching the woman speak for five hours. She was able to keep the group enthralled with stories she had no doubt told for decades. Her approach was simple and somewhat grandmotherly. She was kind and direct. I was in love. Not to mention that watching her do back of the room sales was inspiring.

I didn't get what I came for though. I hadn't really learned anything new. But I was in love. I approached her after everyone had left the class and her grandson had finished packing the few books and videos that hadn't been snatched up by the audience.

"Dottie, I'm Kevin Hogan. I want you to know you have been an inspiration in my career." [See the quotes?]

"Thank you, Kevin." She looked up into my eyes. She was tired. I've been here before. The last person wants to keep you forever. You have been on stage for six hours and you want to find the bed in the hotel and fall flat on your face and have them wake you in 15 hours for breakfast.

"Dottie, I want you to have this." (I hand her my book, *The Psychology of Persuasion*.)

"Thank you, dear." She's being kind, and I think to myself, okay Kevin, her brain is fading. Either ask or get the hell out of here. She has a date with a hotel pillow and you are being as charming as a bottle of mental Drano.

"Dottie, I have one question for you. I have been doing about $1,500 per speech for the last couple of years. It doesn't change. They don't offer more than $2,000. What do you suggest? You tell me, I'll do it. Anything. What is going to take me to the next ($5,000+) level?"

"Have you asked, Kevin?"

"Pardon me?"

"Have you asked for $5,000?"

"Well, not really. I mean . . . no . . . you know, I haven't."

She put her hand on my arm and patted me like I was a little child. [I am the student at the master's knees. I don't know anything. I seek information.]

"Well honey, just ask." (She looked at my book and smiled.) "Just ask."

"Thanks Dottie, I will."

As I walked out of the door on that brisk Minneapolis afternoon I wondered just how stupid I must have looked. Successful author towers over sweet woman asking the dumbest question on the face of the earth. Thank God no one would ever know about this moment.

Fast forward: one month. It's the early winter in 1998. I have a sore throat and a terrible cold. My nose is stuffier than it ever has been in its life. I feel terrible. CNBC is on in the background. The market is not doing well, and I'm not making money today.

The phone rings.

"Who could that be?" I talk to CNBC when no one else is around.

I answer: "Kevin Hogan, can I help you?"

"Is this Dr. Hogan?"

"Yes, it is."

"Oh, you sound terrible. This is Richard Marks ([Not his real name] with the Sales Association [not] their real name either)."

"How can I help you?"

"Well, we were at your web site, and we are looking for a speaker for our winter meeting in Minneapolis. What are you charging nowadays?"

Here it is, Kevin. You spent the last month finishing *Talk Your Way to the Top*. It's over. The book is at Pelican. What are you going to tell this guy? Your voice sounds like hell. You've just yelled at CNBC. You . . . just ask, honey. Just ask . . .

"Five thousand dollars is my fee, but I'd sure like to know more about your group and what you are looking for."

Richard tells me about his group, tells me they want me to talk about "body language" and asks if I will settle on $4,000, which is what his budget is approved for. What's the difference between 4K and 5K anyway? You're working for one hour, Kevin? You moron. It's an hour drive and you are working for an hour . . . Just ask, honey . . . just ask.

"No. My fee is $5,000, and I think I can give you exactly what you are looking for. An hour of massive entertainment combined with an hour of data all happening simultaneously."

"I'll have to check for approval on $5,000. I'll call you back. Thanks, Kevin, we'll talk soon."

I thought to myself, "You stupid moron." (CNBC was running a commercial with Ringo Starr in it . . . I could use a little help from my friends . . . Ringo . . .) "What the heck are you thinking? Guaranteed $4,000. Been paid that once for a full day, never for an hour and you say, $5,000. Idiot. Idiot. Idiot." Sue Herrara talks with Ron

Insana about how the market is taking a hit today, and I'm feeling like a bigger idiot by the microsecond. The phone doesn't ring for the rest of the day.

[Notice the self-deprecation? See how I pick on myself?]

The next day the phone rings. I'm waiting . . .

"Kevin Hogan."

"That really you?"

"Who's this?"

"Richard Marks."

"Hi Richard, good to hear your voice." I'm thinking, I'll take the $4,000. Just offer it again, now, and I'm yours.

"Kevin we got the $5,000 approved and would like you to". . . . and then I hear nothing but Dottie in my mind and I think, "Dottie, I love you . . ." "Just ask, honey". . . . I never doubted you Dottie, I swear . . . just ask . . . and I wrote *The Psychology of Persuasion.* I mean, how long does it take to realize that you are unable to follow your own advice? *Dottie, you are the greatest . . .*

"How does that sound, Kevin?"

"Yes, absolutely, let's run through the details again. My head is foggy from this flu."

Deal closed. Check received in six business days. That was the last time I doubted that still small sweet voice in my head. Dottie is with me always.

Have you ever suffered from low self-esteem? We all do. I tell you this story because every time I think of it I remember that I'm worth an enormous amount to people, to society, to myself. I also think of my childhood because it reminds me that no matter how tough things get, they aren't going to be that bad ever again.

When you sell, *you* determine your outcomes.

Whether you are 10 years old or 70 years old you are going to determine your own fate in selling. You are a free agent and can choose to sell almost any product or service you want. Once you have the product or service picked out that you want to sell, remember this fact: *People don't buy your products, they buy you.*

You must represent a great product or service. What you sell is critical to your self-image and your self-esteem. It needs to be the best, and if it isn't, dump it and go get on the team that is the best. Every product has problems. Every service has its weaknesses. My question is, did you pick the best of the group? If not, go sign up with the best because once you do, the rest of the story is about you!

Selling is an inside job. It all takes place inside of people's minds. Selling is a simple science that encompasses beliefs, values, attitudes, lifestyles, emotions, feelings, and psychological shifts. Selling is the most wonderful profession on earth because it gives you what you want:

- Freedom
- Security
- Productivity
- Independence
- Sense of Accomplishment

No longer are you a slave to anyone. You are your own boss, and you are the master of your life. You'll never work 40 hours again. You'll work 50 or 60 because they are for you and the people you love. Selling is the solution to the destructive "dollars per hour" mentality that exists everywhere. You'll never get paid an hourly wage again. You'll be "unemployed" every day for the rest of your life, and you will never feel more in charge of your own life.

Covert Persuasion Lesson 1. Through the stories in this chapter, I was able to teach you about my dedication to my family when I was a child. You learned that I cared about my family. You learned that I wanted to take care of them.

Covert Persuasion Lesson 2. Through the stories in this chapter you learned my exact process of finally asking to be paid what I am worth. You saw my struggle with my own self-esteem and discovered that you are a lot like me. If I can do it, you can do it. That message was critical to get through from my conscious mind to your unconscious mind.

Covert Persuasion Lesson 3. You now know that I have been successful in the field of influence, and are, therefore, more likely to accept what I tell you as factual, and you are more likely to act upon those messages.

Covert Persuasion Lesson 4. I have disclosed personal weaknesses to you so you know that I am not a superman—nor do I think I am. If you want people to like you and respect you, you must let them know that you are not arrogant. You are just like they are.

8 | Using Questions to Covertly Persuade

I know something about you.

You will answer a question . . . any question . . . every question. You will answer it even if not aloud. You will answer it at least in your own head, even if you don't know the answer.

There is one fundamental truth: people will accept an idea that is the result of their thinking, not yours. The entire trick in persuasion is to help the other person develop his own idea, which, of course, is really your idea. You let him claim it, own it, and then he will act on it.

The ability to own the decision necessarily involves a high level of commitment to the decision, and the only decisions that are carried out or executed (without direct supervision) are the ones that are owned by the person, in which he feels personally responsible.

Irrationality

A few years ago, while in Florida, I discovered an old book at a used bookstore that has become one of my favorites. It's simply titled

Irrationality:Why We Don't Think Straight. I've learned several very important lessons about how you think and how I think. This understanding is critical to the success of any and every persuasion attempt. Today I want to share one important tactic that will help you persuade other people to your way of thinking.

The Availability Factor

This is a simple tactic to persuade the thinking of other people. It's called the *Availability Factor.* The bottom line is that your judgment is clouded by what is most available to you. This is why newspapers and TV news broadcasts can be used as evidence that an opinion is a fact.

This Availability Factor is sometimes referred to as the availability error simply because having some fact, or set of facts that is right there or always available, does not translate into something that is necessarily true or right or correct. It could be wrong or false, but since it is most available to you, you may accept it without questioning it. This is where the power is. This is what advertisers count on; they rely on it to build a brand. They call this *Top of Mind Awareness.* In reality, they are simply trying to make their brand the most available to you.

For example, if an airliner crashes, it will get amazing coverage in the media. Everywhere you turn, you will see the pictures, hear the eyewitness accounts, and see the experts on TV that analyze what happened. The fact remains, however, that flying is still many times safer than driving your car.

Here's an interesting fact. You are statistically more likely to be kicked to death by a donkey than to die in a plane crash. But we don't see or hear very many stories of people dying this way. Rationally speaking, we should have a greater fear of donkeys than airplanes, but we don't because of the Availability Factor.

The Bottom Line

Make your product, service, situation, or opportunity the most available message in your target's field of perception, both in a personal one-on-one conversation and in the wider picture of media and advertising. You might be thinking it sounds pushy to make your product or service the center of attention when talking one-on-one with someone else. It's not. It's all in how you do it. Put simply, carefully turn any mention of a competitor into a conversation about the features and benefits of your particular situation or opportunity. Thus, you simply turn the attention back onto your offer. When you do this, you make your offer more available because that's where the focus is. This will cause him or her to accept it more readily. Being available can be very persuasive!

Questions are so powerful they deserve an entire book by themselves. They may be the ultimate persuasion tool. We'll cover the core aspects of the question and how to use this unique tool to covertly persuade others to your way of thinking. However, we highly recommend that you study this topic further and look to the bibliography in the back and add some of the books listed there to your personal library. There are several excellent books on the power of questions listed.

Questions that have *emotional appeal* and are properly timed make others want to listen. Emotionally power-packed, they command situations, improve personality and persuasion, and help others buy you, your product, and your service.

Covert Power

Of all the structures in the English language, I am most fascinated by the question. It has power. It has simplicity. It can shape, lead, persuade, influence, inform, and accuse. It's an awesome tool.

Psychologically, the question is a power point. By this I mean that if we're in the middle of a conversation and out of the blue someone walks up to us and asks very politely, "Excuse me, what time is it?" we're compelled to answer. We don't simply continue our conversation. We *must* answer this person.

There are some fundamental root causes for our automatic response behavior, and because of these root causes, the question becomes a powerful Covert Persuasion tool.

Foremost among root causes for our automatic-answer behavior are our society and the way we are raised. We are told to be polite, and not answering a question asked of us is rude, inconsiderate, and disrespectful. We actually *want* to answer questions to show we are knowledgeable, to have the attention of everyone on us, and to appear superior. So, we answer all questions asked in our presence; most of them we answer out loud, but all are answered internally.

Internal Questions

There is a starting point for everything, and that includes this process of asking questions. Before you can ask powerful questions of your prospect, you must first be aware of some of the damaging questions you may already be asking yourself, and then resolve to clean all of that up by redirecting your focus off the things you don't want and onto the things that you do want.

Are you asking yourself any of the following dangerous questions?

- Why can't I sell more?
- What is stopping me from being more successful?
- How come everyone always has a problem?
- Why do all the prospects think our price is too high?

- Why do I have to battle with every potential customer?
- Why don't people trust me?
- Why can't I make enough money?
- Why can't I reach my goals?
- Is this really such a great field?

Note that the above questions are self-defeating; they put you in a bad mental state. To get better answers, you need to ask better questions.

What Do Questions Do?

I really believe that the skillful use of questions, when combined with powerful emotional appeals, is among the most effective ways to persuade someone to your point of view and to *want* to take positive action toward the realization of your goals.

If you've ever watched *Law & Order*, or any of the great legal shows on TV that show lawyers arguing their cases in a courtroom in front of a jury, it becomes apparent how important the question chain is in altering options and persuading people.

Lawyers are fascinating to study. Their success or failure ultimately comes down to asking the right questions. They weave a powerful story (often with lots of emotion) with questions asked of the witness that lead the jury's thought process in the specific direction the lawyer wants it to go. Everything is mapped out completely before the day begins, before the first question is asked. This preparation is one critical key to success.

The "Because" Research

You've probably heard about the famous experiment that was conducted by Ellen Langer. She used a college setting where students were in line to use the copier. She sent a person to the front of the line and had him say, "Excuse me, can I go in front of you? I'm in a hurry." About 60 percent of people allowed this person to cut in line and use the copier. However, when the person said, "Excuse me, can I go in front of you because I need to make some copies," almost 95 percent of people allowed this person to go before them. Wow! It was determined that the word "because" was all it took for people to respond like Pavlov's dog. They say "because," and we allow them to cut in line in front of us!

Notice that the all-powerful question was used here. The researchers didn't have the person walk up and say, "I'm going to make my copies now because I have to make some copies." It's when the request for compliance comes in the form of the question that it has maximum power.

The 10 Things Questions Do

There are really 10 fundamental things that questions can do for you when you are Covertly Persuading another person. All of them stem from the basic truth that the person asking the question is in complete control of the exchange.

Don't think this is true? Think about the great TV interviewers like Larry King and Barbara Walters. When they interview someone, they get that person to reveal more information than he planned to reveal. In fact, Barbara Walters' trademark is to dig deep enough with questions and ask them in such an empathetic and caring way that the person opens up and often will cry.

Questions Break Preoccupation and Get Immediate Attention

For better or worse, the simplest question gives you this advantage.

Questions Put Your Listener or Audience on the Defensive

Before replying, your listener has to *think* of an answer. This puts him on the defensive, gains time for you, and gives you the opportunity to organize your next thought or action. The *time* it takes to get answers can be decisively advantageous. You may enlist this time to direct, identify, confuse, delay, save life or property, even change a criminal's mind.

Questions Allow Your Listeners to Speak

People love to do this, especially when they know the answer. This makes the obvious your ally.

Questions Sustain Interest in Your Subject

By stimulating responses, they hold or recapture attention even when your conversation is weakening.

Questions Cut Resistance by Bringing Objections into the Open

By eliminating guesswork, questions shorten the time needed for persuasion. They direct your words and actions toward what is *really* on your listener's mind.

Questions Lead Your Listeners Toward the Conclusion You Want

Example: "Most people are buying the red one while they're still available; you'd probably like a red one too, right?" This is an example of a "leading" question. People will first silently—in their own minds—answer your questions. You are letting your audience lead themselves into the course of action you have been leading them toward. Once they start this process, they will start agreeing. You have entered and directed their minds with questions; your listeners will change their minds with their own answers.

Questions Give Your Listeners Credit for the Thinking

By eliciting replies, you ensure mutuality. Why is that important? Because it proves that you are emotionally reaching your listeners. *Recognition* is powerful and reassuring. Once your listeners reach the conclusion you want them to reach, you can congratulate them on their sharp observations and reasoning skills. People want credit for their thinking. Questions give it to them.

Questions Bypass Distractions

A distraction is a preoccupation breaker that does not help you. Your listener's mind turns toward the distraction. It's up to you to bring it back to the point. Don't fight the distraction—blend into it with a question. A tactful question instantly helps you recapture the attention of your listener(s). Another question or two and you can almost always reactivate the previous high note. To swiftly regain control of situations, bypass distractions with blend-in questions.

For example, when you're asking for the final commitment, and a loud train roars by outside the building and distracts everyone, you simply say, "You can either sit on the tracks and get run over, or you can climb aboard and ride the fast train to the exciting and profitable future!"

Questions Take the Edge off a Direct Command

Don't tell people what to do, ask them. Asking is good emotional appeal; your listener is making the decision. Telling means that you are making the decision. Make your listener feel more important by asking. Why create resistance and conflict by ordering others around?

Questions Build Your Confidence in Yourself

Questions can start a conversation, control one, or suggest a next meeting. Even when unfamiliar subjects arise, your ability to use questions and combine them with emotions will save the day.

Rules for Asking Questions

Just as there are rules for riding a bike, there are rules for asking questions that matter. Not all questions will make a difference in the mind of your listener. You must think through your situation completely first, then begin asking. When we say think it through first, think of the trial lawyer. Questions are his only weapon when questioning a witness in court. He doesn't just think of one question, he thinks of hundreds of questions, and more importantly, puts them in likely "question chains" based on the answers he expects to get to each question. So, take a tip from successful trial lawyers: plan in advance, and follow these rules:

Word Your Question in Such a Way That You Get the Answer You Want

Example: "Wouldn't it be wonderful if you could have more time for relaxation?" This question is designed to elicit a "yes" response and has a self-preservation appeal too.

Be Sure Your Audience Knows the Answer

It bothers people to be asked a question they cannot answer. On the other hand, it is an excellent strategy to ask questions of people in areas in which they can answer. They will love to share their knowledge and help to advance the discussion. It allows the person to feel valued.

However, the main rule still holds true: Only ask questions you already know the answers to. This way you can control the thought direction of everyone involved. This is a covert-control mechanism.

Use Leading Questions Wherever Possible

A leading question puts the answer into your listener's mind and gives double impact to what you are saying. A leading question is easy to work with. You simply make a statement and turn it into a question: "This book is fascinating, isn't it?" Leading questions can be used everywhere. They find their way into advertising, courtrooms, boardrooms, and family rooms. It's really the small *tag question* at the end of the question that makes it into one that begs for agreement.

Objectively Relate Your Question to the Situation, Time, and Listener

Use the situation, context, content, environment, and so forth to connect to your prospect. When your question is connected to the situation, or to your target person, it will be answered more readily. Usually when using this questioning technique your goal is to take the known and relate it to the unknown by linking it with a question. For example, "I know you've always liked the green model, but now for the first time, it's available in red; let's go ahead and send you one, ok?"

Have an Emotional Relationship Built into Your Question

Several emotional appeals are available to choose from, including self-preservation, new experience, recognition, money, and romance. It's absolutely true that everyone wants to be healthy, happy, and perceived as an important contributor; so, attach your product, service, or idea to one of these very self-centered emotional hooks. For example,

"Can you imagine how much people will admire you when they see you driving around town in this new car?"

Use a "Choice Question" When You Want Definite Action or Agreement

Offer a choice of agreeing one way or agreeing another way. "When do you prefer delivery, at the beginning of next week or before this weekend?" Use of this rule for choice questions requires a little practice, but you will find it surprisingly persuasive.

Questions Clarify Your Thinking

Every single successful persuasion attempt starts with you. You must start in your own head. You must be completely clear about what outcome you desire. To help that internal picture develop, ask yourself the following questions:

- How do I want to feel when I'm through with this conversation?
- What do I want my target to feel?
- What is my selfish goal? (What exactly do I really want out of this exchange?)
- How long will it take? (How much of my time? How much of my target's time?)
- Will I be closer to my goal if my target agrees to my request?
- Will my target be better off as a result of his willing cooperation?
- What are the specifics? (dates, times, costs, etc.)
- Who else do I need to involve?

- What don't I know?

- What could go wrong?

- What are the objections I'm likely to hear from my target?

- What are the benefits my target will enjoy as a result?

- Is this really worth involving another person, or should I just do it myself?

The above list is a great starting point. It is just the beginning of the kind of precontact thought homework that will make your persuasion attempt successful. Just imagine, if you actually write out these types of questions, and then force yourself to focus on them and answer each one, you'll be almost unstoppable. There's really nothing your target can do that you didn't predict. Plus, with your complete answers will come the power of a crystal-clear goal. This will allow you to use a forced focus to keep your mind and actions on the attainment of your goal. All your persuasion attempts will be much more successful.

Questions Involve Your Target

There is absolutely no substitute for a well-timed, skillfully asked question. It will immediately involve the mind of your target and the real covert power is the ability to direct thought using questions. For example, if I ask you, "Excuse me, I need to catch a plane, could you tell me exactly what time it is?" For the next several seconds, I will successfully direct your thoughts onto your watch (or some clock in the room). In any event, by asking this simple question, I have taken control of your brain, even if only for a couple of seconds.

Here are some questions to prompt the thinking of your target:

- Would you like to enjoy (benefit of your request)?

- Have you ever wondered how to get (outcome you believe they would desire)?

- What's important to you in X? (This question tells you their criteria. You'll use the answer they give you later to help draw them into your way of thinking).

- How much better would work be if (goal of yours)?

- Think of how impressed everyone will be when you (comply with your request).

It's All in How You Ask

There is proof that how you ask a particular question will dramatically change the outcome. For example, in 1984 Kahneman and Tversky performed some experimental research with results that proved the power of the question.

The experiment asked participants to imagine that preparations were under way to handle an outbreak of a disease that was expected to kill 600 people. There were two alternative programs proposed to help the situation. In the first program, called "A," 200 people would be saved. In the second program, called "B," there was a one-third probability that no people would be saved.

Next, participants were told two additional options were available. Program "C" would result in 400 people dying. Program "D" provided for a one-third probability that nobody would die and a two-thirds probability that all 600 people would die.

What program do you think people picked? When you look closely, you'll notice that Programs A and C are identical and so are B and D. However, 72 percent of the people chose the "sure thing" (program A) over the "risky gamble" (program B). However—and this is the key part—researchers obtained the opposite result when the question was framed the opposite way (C, D).

In other words, someone who chooses A should logically choose C. Someone who chooses B should logically choose D because they give the exact same result. But the different framing or perspective of the question shifts people's thinking in a dramatic way.

$10,000 COVERT PERSUASION TRICK

People are not logical or rational when they make decisions; they are irrational! So, become aware of the irrational and use that as the reason to comply.

Asking about the Future

A truly covert technique that absolutely persuades people to buy your product or service is a future pace. This works by mentally walking the person into the future, a future that is without the benefits you can provide (or a future in which they do not do what you want them to do). Help them to experience the pain associated with not choosing to do *the right thing* (your goal). Paint this picture graphically, and take it to the realistic extreme. Mention how they will be in a worse position. You may want to add details about how other people they respect will view them in this pretend future, how they will face disapproval or possibly cause others they care about to feel some discomfort, embarrassment, or harm.

Then slowly remind them that none of that has happened yet, and that you can help them to prevent any of it from ever happening if they choose differently right now. You can offer them a better choice in the present that will not lead to all of those bad outcomes. In other words, you (or the course of action you want the other person to take) are the solution to their situation.

Then, once you've done these steps, ask them which they would prefer. The choice will be obvious. They will choose you.

9

Using Emotions to Covertly Persuade

I'm sure you've heard it said that people make decisions emotionally first, *then* justify with fact. This is absolutely true. We are emotional. Emotions guide our every waking moment. We do not think logically; although in many decisions logic plays a role, it's always a *secondary* role. Emotions are powerful, and consciously using them to your advantage is *covert* because the strength, power, and control of emotion is largely a subconscious process that completely bypasses the critical thinking of the vast majority of people.

We rarely think about how we feel when something happens in our life. We just *feel* it. We simply react *emotionally* to our environment. This is where the power lies for you in the persuasion game. Before you can attempt to use the power of emotions, you must first truly understand your target's goals. Without correctly knowing this, any prediction you make about how your target will react to a given stimulus will likely be wrong.

"The aim of the wise is not to secure pleasure, but to avoid pain."
—Aristotle

The Power of Emotions to Connect and Covertly Persuade People

I was recently at a large meeting of business people where we heard a guest speaker from Habitat for Humanity. The organization could have simply asked the audience to donate time, money, and materials to help in the construction efforts, and they would have received some donations. But that's not what they did. Instead, the speaker told a story of the Nelson family (not their real name) in great detail. She told us about their jobs and their struggles. She told us about their daughter Sara (not her real name either). Sara was six years old and for her entire life had slept with her parents in the one-bedroom apartment where they had lived for the past six years.

As you may know, the day a Habitat home is turned over to the family, there is a big celebration with a ribbon cutting, and all the volunteers that worked on the home are present. As the story was told, the big day came and the home was turned over to the grateful, tearful parents. But something was missing—Sara. So several people started looking for her and our speaker found her. Sara was in one of the bedrooms of the new house, sitting on the floor in the middle of the empty room, crying. When asked why she was crying, her lips were trembling as she answered, "Is this really my room?" Sara went on to say how beautiful it was and that she couldn't believe this was happening.

By the time the story was finished, several people were moved to tears. Yes, the Habitat organization could have simply asked for donations, and they would have received some. However, pulling on the heartstrings in this very emotional way resulted in a deeper impact on the audience. That story has generated more volunteers and secured a bright future for more of the Sara Nelsons in the world.

You can see that using emotion to persuade is far more powerful than using facts. This is true because facts are cold and unfeeling. Emotions carry the meaning and can move people to take the action you want. However, just like the Outcome-Based Thinking we talked about earlier, it is absolutely critical that we have that crystal clear picture of exactly what it is we want the other person(s) to do. It can be dangerous to stir up a lot of raw emotion if you don't have a plan of where to direct that energy. Make sure you have a plan. That way, when you've connected with them emotionally, it becomes clear to them what must be done (and that just happens to be the thing that you want done: the donation, the vote, the purchase, etc).

The Uniqueness of Emotions

Emotions happen first and literally guide the logic side of the brain. The path of thought is always emotion, *then* logic. If you want to have the ability to persuade by using emotions, then do your homework. Carefully choose exactly what emotions you intend to touch and know exactly where that will lead your target. If you want to reduce the negative emotional response someone has, you need to evoke positive emotion in the other person first, and then tie that to your persuasion attempt.

$10,000 COVERT PERSUASION TRICK
People decide emotionally, then justify with facts. Build a lot of emotion into your argument, follow that with the word "because," and then give a fact. This formula works!

We Are Emotional, Then Logical

The statements outlined below are unfortunately true, and at first glance make it difficult to change people's minds. But look closely at them.

$10,000 COVERT PERSUASION TRICK
People only seek evidence that supports their existing beliefs. So, starting from what you know they believe, give them something they "know" is true and then expand that toward your ultimate goal. This allows them to agree while saving face.

$10,000 COVERT PERSUASION TRICK
Push-Back Effect: When a person is emotionally committed to a belief, contrary opinions are usually pushed back and only end up strengthening people's original belief. They end up more convinced that they are right. Knowing this, don't push. Instead, give them new information by asking them questions to get them to draw their own new conclusions. These conclusions will obviously be ones designed to help you.

If this is true, and it is, then what hope do we have of persuading the other person that our way is the *right* way? A good covert persuader will identify with the position of the other and use a *feel, felt, found* technique to give the other person a small bit of new information to grab onto, which allows him to begin thinking in your direction while saving face.

For example, it may sound like this: "I understand how you feel about that, a lot of people I've met once felt the same way, but what they found out when they looked closer was . . ."

This technique works very covertly in your personal, business, and social life. It works because a couple of key psychological elements are at work. First, it lets people know that a group of similar others thought as they are now thinking (this is social proof and makes them feel at ease and takes their defenses down). Next, it gives them a brand new piece of information. It allows their brain to say to themselves, "If I'd known that, things would be different now." And this new piece of information allows the person to begin to move his thinking more in line with yours. It seems rational to conform to the social norm. This is a very, very covertly persuasive tactic.

There is another emotional reaction that, if well understood, can turn the person to your way of thinking and help you get your way more often.

$10,000 COVERT PERSUASION TRICK

People will take personal credit for successes but blame failures on the situation or other people. People don't like to admit they are wrong. Structure your argument so they don't ever have to admit they were wrong.

This is really an appeal to ego (which, of course, is all irrational emotion). Most people will not accept personal blame for a bad outcome. Instead, they will look for someone or something to blame it on. As a covert persuader, you must help them to find that someone or something, and then appeal to the strength and power of their intent. Let them know that you know they would have done things differently if they had been in total control. Then, show them how doing what you want done will help them to claim a big personal victory and credit for a huge success.

$10,000 COVERT PERSUASION TRICK

People are irrationally and emotionally influenced by certainty.

Phrasing your request to emphasize certainty influences the likelihood that they will comply with your request, regardless of the logic.

People want certainty. Surprises on this deep level of psychology are not welcome. We like to know what's going on. When you phrase your request for compliance so that it gives them a true feeling of certainty of an outcome, they'll likely follow you.

"Thinking is the hardest work there is, which is probably why so few engage in it."

—Henry Ford

10

27 Observations About People

And How to Covertly Persuade Them

This chapter contains 27 observations about how people think and behave in various situations in life and business. In the lessons ahead, we'll share an observation we've drawn from our business—selling—and general life experiences and then relate it to a Covert Persuasion Tactic or Trick.

What follows are 27 lessons we've learned from our decades of life experience in business and in the field of selling to real customers who sometimes buy and sometimes don't. We'll not only share our observation with you, but we'll also connect them to a real Covert Persuasion Technique that you can use to help each situation turn out more in your favor—and get your way!

Lesson 1: People Don't Know How to Ask Great Questions

You know that most people have a hard time asking great questions. They prefer to pretend they already know.

How to Covertly Persuade: Since people want to be perceived as already knowing the answer to any given situation, you'll help them share their expertise by answering questions you've previously thought of to help guide their thinking to your point of view. Refer back to Chapter 8 and spend some time working on the quality and persuasiveness of your questions. Your increased ability to ask great questions of other people will ultimately lead them to make great decisions, the decisions you want them to make.

Lesson 2: Attitude Manipulates Experience

You know that you must be consciously aware of the impact of your attitude on how you view any event in life. It's critical. Your target person is the same way. His bad attitude will cloud his current experience.

How to Covertly Persuade: Injecting a powerful state-breaking question into your conversation can alter the other person's view of the situation and improve his attitude. Your challenge in life is to accept the responsibility to control and choose your own attitude, while at the same time using all you know to improve the attitudes and moods of all those around you.

Lesson 3: People Need Help to Visualize

You know that people are actually very good at visualizing. It's just the word that sometimes throws them off. Questions help your target person to picture the final situation.

How to Covertly Persuade: Ask more questions to lead people to a new understanding. Use word pictures. Use metaphors and analogies to connect the new product, situation, or event with something the customer is very familiar with. This will help the picture become clearer.

Lesson 4: People Know What They Don't Want

Become aware that most people will be quick to say what they don't want. The reality is they do know what they want. They just aren't sure how to express it. This is where you help.

How to Covertly Persuade: An excellent phrase to remember is: "I know you don't know, but if you did know, what would it be?" A surprisingly high number of people will answer this question clearly. Remember, your ability to ask clear, well-thought–out questions of your target person at this point will help you (and your target) understand what it is you and he *do* want. When done skillfully, what they want will line up perfectly with what you need them to do.

Lesson 5: Speed is the Key to Getting the Job

Sometimes what matters most often is "How quick can I have it?" Speed is key.

How to Covertly Persuade: Look closely at the way you're doing things now. Ask yourself some powerful questions like: "What are seven ways I can get it done faster?" Force yourself to come up with seven answers. Chances are very good that if you can provide it faster, you'll win more cooperation, trust, respect, and more business. The next critical component is communicating that advantage to your customer. One easy way to do this is the alternate-choice question. If you can truly provide faster service, then the two alternatives will be very close, both closer than he or she expects, and very impressive. You'll win the business without having to make unbelievable claims.

Lesson 6: People Just Don't Come Back

The unfortunate truth is that most people would rather leave without confronting you about a bad experience with your company. The thought of complaining may put them in a bad state.

How to Covertly Persuade: You must develop the ability to become super-sensitive to the treatment your customers are receiving. You must be their advocate. And, of course, you must make every upset customer feel that you are really listening. How? By asking open-ended questions and listening. Do not interrupt the customer or try to answer or explain every point. Simply let them be heard. Then, reassure them you value their business and would like to make things right for them. However, before offering what you think is the solution to the problem, ask the customers what they think would make the situation better. You just might be surprised.

Lesson 7: Squeaky Wheel Syndrome

Sometimes in business the complainer is satisfied whether or not there is any merit to his complaint.

How to Covertly Persuade: Questioning the complainer sometimes puts him or her on the defensive and the situation can get worse. Never question their intent. The only valuable questions at this point are those designed to gain more information. Listen. Then act to make the situation better for the customer.

Lesson 8: Customers Don't Know the Solution; You Do

Your clients are every bit as busy as you are every day. Therefore, they don't have the time to study your products and services and figure out how they can best be used to solve their problems—that's your job.

How to Covertly Persuade: Once you've asked enough questions and really listened to the answers, *confidently recommend*! Your authority has now been sufficiently built to the point where your recommendation will carry influence with the other person. Use it.

Lesson 9: People Just Don't Question Things Enough

People habitually fail to ask fresh questions. You also heard the old saying, *beware the unquestioned conviction.* This is advice to keep you aware of possibility in your surroundings.

How to Covertly Persuade: Be the ethical provocateur; ask, "What would happen if . . . ?" more often. Question the status quo.

Lesson 10: People Have Internal Gauges

Like a dashboard on a car, we each have internal gauges. These gauges let us know when something is not right. They sometimes warn us of danger. The reaction by the customer is sometimes confusing to us, but it is always in line with, and as a direct result of, their own internal gauges. The goal in selling is to get all the internal gauges of the prospect or customer to line up with the decision to buy!

How to Covertly Persuade: Understand that you also have internal gauges, and asking questions is the only way to make sure each person is reading the other correctly.

Lesson 11: People are Like Pigs, Oranges, and Corn

The unfortunate truth is that as far as economic or market value is concerned, most people are like a commodity. They are like pigs, oranges, or corn. Each orange is like the other. All the same.

How to Covertly Persuade: First, work on yourself. Realize that you don't have to be a commodity. Work on developing your own, personal Unique Selling Proposition (USP). Then help those you care about to do the same. Developing a USP will add clarity to your life and help you to become successful faster. Once you know what makes you unique, you are no longer like all the rest. You are no longer a commodity. You stand out from the ordinary and have more persuasive power because of it.

Lesson 12: Send the Time Wasters to Your Competition

The 80/20 rule is the core lesson here. The harsh reality is that many customers aren't worth spending your valuable time with; send them away. You'll frustrate your competitor, and free up time to concentrate on the top 20 percent of your clients.

How to Covertly Persuade: Train yourself first, then your entire staff on how to recognize these time-wasters, then how to politely refer them to your competitor. This training will be very profitable.

Lesson 13: People Feel Entitled

This mentality is undeniable. It's everywhere. Simply visit any customer service department anywhere and listen to the way people talk to each other. Unfortunately, it's all too common that customers have to gear themselves up for a fight. People approach businesses these days with a *you owe me!* attitude.

How to Covertly Persuade: Step up to the plate with real, honest treatment in response to the questions you get from your customers.

Lesson 14: Perception is Reality

The way you see the world *is* the world (as far as you're concerned). Your prospect or customer also views the world from his vantage point and usually has an entirely different read on things. The cause of all miscommunication is this differing view of the world and what it means.

How to Covertly Persuade: The success you have in communicating with others will depend on how well you can see the world from their point of view. You must develop questions, the answers to which will bring you closer to an understanding of the world from the other person's point of view. This will clear up the communication.

Lesson 15: People are Lazy

It's basic human nature to take the easy road. If it's easier not to do something, and there is no punishment or it's meaningless, then it's most likely that the person will not do it. This could mean that if it's easier not to buy from you, or if there are no consequences for not buying from you, then there will be no sale.

How to Covertly Persuade: Clearly show your Unique Selling Proposition and how buying now will help customers to avoid a costly, painful problem. Then, and most importantly, make it easy for them to buy. Do everything for them. Remember, people are lazy. If you require your prospects to do many things, they will very likely never become your customers.

Lesson 16: People Do More to Avoid Pain Than They Will Do to Gain Pleasure

Pain is a bigger motivator than pleasure. Even though, as a group, salespeople seem to be a pleasure-seeking bunch, there is a stronger motivator behind outstanding sales performance, and many times it is a fear of poverty, fear of failure, fear of embarrassment, or some other type of uncomfortable, or painful experience that is at the root of all behavior of the supersuccessful.

How to Covertly Persuade: Show the absolute risk of loss—show what the person will absolutely lose if he doesn't take action now. Conversely, show him how buying your product or service now will not only avoid that pain but will give him some bonus pleasure. When you do this, you'll be much more likely to get the sale. Sometimes, actually writing your argument out on paper first is a smart thing to do; you'll be amazed at the very profitable results if you actually get out some paper and a pen and do this.

Lesson 17: Work Fills the Time Allowed

People have an amazing ability to make one hour's worth of work fill an entire afternoon or to make a full day's workload fit into one single afternoon. Work fills the time allowed for it.

How to Covertly Persuade: Help others establish time frames for each separate task. This way, the maximum amount of work will be accomplished. It's up to you. Remember, the best way to do this is through skillful questioning.

Lesson 18: People Don't Listen, They Wait to Talk

You've learned how *most* people do not actively listen to all of what you're saying. Unfortunately, this is probably true for you as well. Be aware. Listen. You can't learn anything by talking. Listen to others.

How to Covertly Persuade: Use the "interest noises" to convey interest and to encourage the other person to talk more. Use questions to steer the conversation. Listen more than you talk.

Lesson 19: People Don't Laugh Enough

Laughter is important. It's healthy. Not laughing suppresses the immune system and actually shortens your life. So, "lighten up" and "laugh it off."

How to Covertly Persuade: Watch your kids closely. They laugh naturally. They're not waiting to see if the boss (parent) laughs first, or whether or not it's politically correct to laugh. No, they just burst out laughing. It's spontaneous. The best way to relearn this is to be around kids more. Learn from them. On this point, they're the experts.

Lesson 20: Negative People Infect Others. Avoid Them

This can be a difficult lesson to learn. Some people never learn it. You must disassociate yourself from those people who are chronically negative and down. Leave them behind. Avoid them. Move on.

How to Covertly Persuade: Take a hard look at the people who are in your life on a daily basis. Are there any constantly negative people around you? You know what to do.

Lesson 21: A Limited Vocabulary Limits Your Life

It can be like a life sentence. The difference is you hold the keys to the cell. Words are the keys. Words are powerful. Words can set you free and make every experience in life rich and vibrant.

How to Covertly Persuade: Commit to increasing your habitual vocabulary. Find new words. Buy a good dictionary and thesaurus and refer to them often. Trick: Whenever you see a word you don't understand in a book, on the Internet, in an article, *look it up!* Find out what it means, learn and use the word yourself to burn it into memory. Set yourself up on a schedule to learn a couple of new words every day of your life—and commit to actually using them to increase the richness of your life.

Lesson 22: People Overpromise and Underdeliver

You learned that companies might have good intentions but usually fall short of making the customer feel valued. They promise a lot to entice you to do business with them, and then they deliver far less, leaving us feeling cheated.

How to Covertly Persuade: Commit to running your life the way this old cliché was meant to be stated, "underpromise and overdeliver!" That will serve you well, and you'll be very successful. Word of mouth will spread like wildfire.

Lesson 23: Peer Pressure Doesn't End with High School

The lesson here was simple. *People like to be like the people they like.* We know this is true.

How to Covertly Persuade: This is where we can use the law of association and the law of friends to help us persuade others to our cause. Show others that by doing what you suggest, they will be like someone they like and respect. They'll act.

Lesson 24: Most People Lack a Burning Desire

Wouldn't it be great to literally jump out of bed in the morning full of energy and anxious to meet the day and do fun things and make a difference? You can.

How to Covertly Persuade: Spend some time doing a structured goal-setting workshop. If you've never done this, do it. It will streamline your life and give you direction and purpose. You'll begin to see things clearly for the first time. People, situations, and events will either be in line with your selfish goal, or clearly a distraction. This clarity is power. You'll become many times more successful when you develop your burning desire.

Lesson 25: People Just Don't Anticipate. They React

You learned the power of becoming a *"professional anticipator."* Know your plan B *before* you need it. You may never need it, but if you do, you'll be poised to act instead of react.

How to Covertly Persuade: Use paper and pen and think ahead to the next step. Next week, next month, next year . . . think of all the possibilities. What could happen? What's likely to happen? Then form plans to take advantage of situations as they develop. If you actually do this, you'll be a success.

Lesson 26: Most People Point Out Why it Won't Work

You learned that the devil's advocate is a person who does not create and only destroys. Nothing was ever created by a devil's advocate. Avoid these people.

How to Covertly Persuade: Challenge these people on the spot. Their negative energy can be contagious. Stop them. How? By asking questions. Ask them for their ideas on how to make the project work. They'll be stumped. They'll be exposed as shallow and without substance. They'll be much quieter when confronted.

Lesson 27: People Don't Read

You've learned the importance of building your own personal library. Reading is learning from the best. Why don't people read? They'd rather be right than curious. Cultivate your curiosity.

How to Covertly Persuade: Buy the books. Listen to the tapes. Attend the seminars. Learn. Soak it all up. Become more curious with every passing day. Discover how things interrelate. Read. Be an example.

> *"There is nothing that is a more certain sign of insanity than to do the same thing over and over and expect the results to be different."*
> —Albert Einstein

11 | Putting It All Together

N ow it's time to put all of this information together in a way that works for you. To recapture the core information in one place, we've created a quick-reference summary in this chapter along with a worksheet that you can fill out to make sure your next persuasive attempt is as successful as possible

Remember, the fundamental goal of Covert Persuasion is to move your target person from where he is to where you want him to be with his cooperation. We call this "Decision Direction."

Let's map this out. If we are observant, we will be fairly accurate in assessing where the other person is at the beginning of any persuasion attempt. And, using outcome-based thinking, we know where we want to end up, and chances are good that we want to persuade him to our way of thinking in as little time as possible.

On the next page is a short decision tree. At every point is a decision. Our goal through the use of the covert persuasion tricks and techniques in this book is to control and direct the decisions the other person makes so that you get more of what you want more often.

Let's look at the diagram in Figure 11.1.

From the picture, you can see that at every step there are a lot of possible decisions your target person can make. You, of course, want him to follow the course that leads to *your* desired outcome. At any step along the way, he could make the wrong decision. This is exactly why you'll want to keep this book at your side or within easy reach. You'll want to stay familiar with all the Covert Persuasion tricks and techniques.

Usually, persuading someone else is not a one-step magic process, although there are some times and conditions when one well-placed technique can absolutely be the answer. But more often than not, you'll have to do some "backward thinking." In other words, start your thinking from the goal you want to accomplish and then work back to the present, where you are now. This will take an extra effort, but will pay off in a seemingly easy success in Covert Persuasion. The other person won't have any

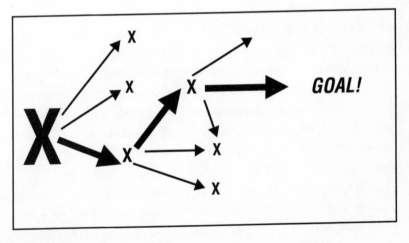

FIGURE 11.1 Decision Making Using Covert Persuasion Tricks and Techniques.

conscious idea what just happened. He will feel ownership of the decisions he comes to (but you will know that you were in the driver's seat). And as we know, people will be more committed to decisions they make than anything you tell them. So, leading your target to your goal using Covert Persuasion Techniques is the key to success.

A Word about Decisions—for You

There is only one way to decide. Just do it. Then, put all of your efforts behind your decision and move ahead with force and focus. Don't look back. Burn the ships and bomb the bridges that brought you to this point. There is no turning back. Once a decision is made, fully commit to its completion.

Once you make a difficult decision, you'll feel better. You can commit all your focus to the direction of the new decision. There is economy and speed in the momentum of a decision.

If it happens that you find yourself on the fence, unable to make a decision, you will experience increasing levels of stress. The longer you put off making the decision—the more you procrastinate—the more you'll feel uncomfortable, uneasy, and unsure.

An inability to decide begins a cycle that creates stress and uses valuable energy. It creates worry, stress, and avoidance behavior. Because you'll avoid and procrastinate, you'll create more worry and stress. Soon this picture in your mind becomes so destructive and negative that you will want to avoid it even more. More procrastination follows. It's a never-ending cycle.

The only way to break out of this cycle is to make a decision and commit to it. Only then will worry and stress melt away. You'll find everything appears clearer, easier, and more exciting. So, decide and commit.

Note: Did you notice that I used a version of the Future-Pace technique that was discussed earlier? I took you into the future of what a lack of decision does—creates worry and stress—and then brought you back to the present and told you the solution is to decide! I then told you that having made a decision will melt away worry and stress, and you'll be back to a state where you will have helped to satisfy a fundamental core human drive for tranquility. Do you see how all of this works together?

Following this chapter is an Appendix of Covert Persuasion Worksheets. These have been put together to help you capture all the important concepts in this book and put them to practical use in your next persuasion situation. These pages will help you make all the preliminary decisions so that you know exactly how to help your target person make the right decisions to end up at *your goal!* Refer directly to these sheets when you have an important sales presentation, interview, union negotiation, or business transaction coming up that you must make go your way. The worksheets lead you through each of the parts of the Covert Persuasion process and help you to make sure you are as persuasive as possible when it counts.

You have our permission to photocopy the Covert Persuasion Worksheet pages so that you can use them each and every time a new situation develops.

A Final Thought

You want to win. You want to improve your positions and conditions in life. Because this is fundamentally true, commit to learning the content of this book. Let it be a starting point for you to become intensely curious about other people. This topic is far more complex than any one book can cover. When you begin to develop an appetite for this subject, it won't be long until you develop your own personal library of books, tapes, CDs, and DVDs about persuasion that will grow into the thousands. Does that sound far-fetched? Both of the authors have personal libraries that contain thousands of titles. We're truly intensely curious about people and how the world works. We encourage you to develop a real, true, burning curiosity to find out more about people. Remember, everything you get in life you will get with and through other people. Curiosity is your strongest ally!

Appendix

Covert Persuasion Worksheet

This worksheet is provided for your use. You have our permission to copy these worksheet pages only, so that you can use this as a checklist and guide for your important persuasion situations. When you completely fill out this worksheet, you'll have a much higher likelihood of success! Go!

Today's Date: _____   **Date of Meeting:** _____

My Selfish Goal (No one sees this but you, so be honest. Write out exactly what you want as a perfect outcome.)

_____

_____

_____

_____

OBT *Outcome-Based–Thinking* **Box**

List of everyone involved: **Where are they starting from:**

1. _____   _____

2. _____   _____

3. _____   _____

4. _____   _____

5. _____   _____

What I want them to believe, feel, and/or do as a result of my persuasion:

1. _____

2. _____

3. _____

4. _____

5. _____

Choose the words, questions, and stories to deliver your message.

WORD MENU   Use as many of the following words as fit naturally in your message; these are the words proven to be among the most persuasive. Circle the ones you plan on using:

You	Money	Save	Love
Results	Health	Easy	Discovery
Proven	New	Safety	Guarantee
Free	Yes	Fast	Why
How	Secrets	Sale	Power
Now	Because	Attention	Announcing
Compare	Complete	Discount	Free
Bargain	Exclusive	Imagine	Magic
Original	Unlimited	Please	Authentic

Acclaimed, Advancement, Amazing, Announcing, Appealing, At Last, Attention, Authentic, Aware, Bargain, Because, Boosts, Breakthrough, Challenge, Change, Choice, Classic, Comfortable, Compare, Complete, Convenient, Delivers, Deserve, Discount, Discover, Discovery, Distinguished, Easy, Easily, Effective, Energy, Exceptional, Exciting, Exclusive, Experience, Experienced, Expert, Extraordinary, Fast, Free, Fresh, Fun, Guarantee, Heal, Help, Honest, How To, Hurry, Imagine, Important, Improved, Indispensable, Incredible, Informative, Instantly, Intimate, Introducing, Irresistible, Last Chance, Love, Luxurious, Magic, Miracle, Money, Money-making, Money-saving, Natural, Naturally, New, Now, Offer, Original, Overcome, Peace of Mind, Perfect, Please, Pleasure, Plus, Popular, Power, Powerfully, Practical, Prevents, Price reduction, Profitable, Promise, Proven, Quickly, Realize, Recommended, Refreshing, Relax, Reliable, Relief, Relieve, Remarkable, Research, Results, Risk Free, Revolutionary, Romantic, Safety, Sale, Satisfaction, Save, Scientific, Secret, Security, Sensational, Service, Simplifies, Soothe, Special Offer, Status, Stop, Stimulating, Striking, Stylish, Superior, Surefire, Surprising, Thank You, Timely, The Truth About, Traditional, Trusted, Ultimate, Unlimited, Unusual, Useful, Valuable, Wanted, Warning, You, Yours

QUESTION CHECKLIST Use these more sparingly. A well-asked, emotion-based question will completely direct the thinking of the other person.

Check your mind for positive internal questions—sometimes negativity creeps in!

How do I want to feel when I have finished this conversation?

What do I want my target to feel?

What is my selfish goal? (What exactly do I really want out of this exchange?)

How long will it take? (How much of my time; how much of my target's time?)

Will I be closer to my goal if my target agrees to my request?

Will my target be better off as a result of his willing cooperation?

What are the specifics? (dates, times, costs, etc.)

Who else do I need to involve?

What don't I know?

What could go wrong?

What are the objections I'm likely to hear from my target?

What are the benefits my target will enjoy as a result?

Is this really worth involving another person or should I just do it myself?

Use "because" in your question. "Because" provides an implicit reason for doing or not doing a certain thing.

Using questions forces answers. Remember that when you ask a question, you are in control of the thought processes of the other person. You can control and direct him by asking the right questions.

PATTERN-INTERRUPTING QUESTIONS
Leading Questions usually end in: ". . . isn't it?" or, ". . . right?"

USING THE HYPNOTIC LANGUAGE PATTERNS

I wouldn't tell you to . . . _____

How do you go about deciding . . . _____

You might want to . . . now . . . _____

What is it that helps you know whether you . . . _____

You don't have to . . . _____

Why is it that some people . . . _____

I don't know if . . . _____

Would you like to see . . . _____

Some people . . . _____

If you could have . . . _____

If you would choose . . . _____

Have you ever seen . . . _____

Would you be surprised if I told you . . . _____

Imagine what would happen if . . . _____

Are you interested in . . . _____

If I could show you a way to . . . _____

What would it be like if you had . . . _____

You may not know . . . _____

Can I show you . . . _____

I'm wondering if . . . _____

Don't think that . . . _____

Don't you feel . . . _____

Using these language patterns successfully depends not on simply saying them, but more on *how you say them.*

Use tonal marking and pausing to make your point covertly.

Write below the sentences you're going to use when you Covertly Persuade your target:

_____

_____

_____

_____

_____

The 55 Covert Persuasion Tactics
Circle the Ones You Are Going to Use

Rapidly build resonant rapport	Use content to build rapport	Use processes to build rapport	Synchronize with your target	Synchronize voices
Synchronize breathing	Synchronize posture and body movement	Testing synchronization	Alter the tone, pace and pitch of your voice	Induce reciprocity
Make the damaging admission	Share part of you with them	The common enemy	Short story about "them"	Give respect
Knock their socks off	Give more than you promised	Use understatement power	Be precise, then beat precision	Faster, easier, better
Be on the edge of your seat	Ask for compliance	Induce a sense of scarcity	Open the door to a friend	Associate the known/unknown
Feel part of the group	Create contrast	Don't ask why	Shift time reference	Unshakable credibility
Use space	Commitment and consistency	Covert hypnotic language patterns	Make body and words say the same thing	Outcome based thinking
Determine how they represent information	Feel, felt, found	Deletion, distortion, generalization	Note-taking	Lower your voice
80/20 rule and Covert Persuasion	Inoculation to persuade	Flexibility	Covertly empathetic mind	Artfully vague language
Power of three	Vocal stress in delivery	Experiential involvement	Persuading with attitude	Using music to persuade
Inconsistency	Fewer choices means more yeses	People believe what they say, not what you say	Be private in public	Oscillation at the decision point

Bibliography

Alesandra, Tony, and Michael J. O'Connor. *The Platinum Rule: Do Unto Others as They'd Like Done unto Them.* New York: Warner Books, 1996.

Anastasi, Tom. *Personality Selling, Selling the Way Customers Want to Buy.* New York: Sterling Publications, 1992.

Anderson, C. A., M.R. Lepper, and L. Ross. "Perseverance of Social Theories: The Role of Explanation in the Persistence of Discredited Information. *Journal of Personality and Social Psychology* 39 (1980): 1039–1049.

Andreas, Steve, and Charles Faulkner. *NLP: The New Technology of Achievement.* New York: William Morrow, 1994.

Aronson, Elliott. *The Social Animal.* New York: W. H. Freeman, 1995.

Belsky, Gary, and Thomas Gilovich. *Why Smart People Make Big Money Mistakes and How to Correct Them.* New York: Fireside, 1999.

Bethel, William. *10 Steps to Connecting With Your Customer: Communication Skills for Selling Your Products, Services, and Ideas.* Chicago: The Dartnell Corporation, 1995.

Bloom, Howard. *The Lucifer Principle: A Scientific Expedition Into the Forces of History.* New York: Atlantic Monthly Press, 1995.

Brodie, Richard. *Virus of the Mind: The New Science of the Meme.* Walnut Creek, CA: Integral Press, 1996.

Brooks, Michael. *Instant Rapport: The NLP Program that Creates Intimacy, Persuasiveness, Power!* New York: Warner Books, 1989.

Brooks, Michael. *The Power of Business Rapport: Use NLP Technology to Make More Money, Sell Yourself and Your Product, and Move Ahead in Business.* New York: HarperCollins, 1991.

Buzan, Tony, and Richard Israel. *Brain Sell.* Brookfield, VT: Gower, 1995.

Cialdini, Robert B. *Influence: Science and Practice.* New York: William Morrow, 1993.

Cohen, Allan R., and David L. Bradford. *Influence Without Authority.* New York: John Wiley & Sons, 1991.

Dalet, Kevin, with Emmett Wolfe. *Socratic Selling: How to Ask the Questions That Get the Sale.* Chicago: Irwin Professional Publishing, 1996.

Dawson, Roger. *Secrets of Power Persuasion: Everything You'll Ever Need to Get Anything You'll Ever Want.* Englewood Cliffs, NJ: Prentice-Hall, 1992.

Dayton, Doug. *Selling Microsoft: Sales Secrets from Inside the World's Most Successful Company.* Holbrook, MA: Dayton, 1997.

Decker, Bert. *You've Got to Be Believed to Be Heard: Reach the First Brain to Communicate in Business and in Life.* New York: St. Martin's Press, 1992.

Dillard, James and Michael Pfau. *The Persuasion Handbook: Developments in Theory and Practice.* Thousand Oaks, CA: Sage Publications, 2004.

Farber, Barry J., and Joyce Wycoff. *Breakthrough Selling: Customer-Building Strategies from the Best in the Business.* Englewood Cliffs, NJ: Prentice-Hall, 1992.

Forgas, Joseph P., and Kipling D. Williams. *Social Influence: Direct and Indirect Processes.* Philadelphia: Psychology Press, 2001.

Gass, Robert, and John Seiter. *Persuasion, Social Influence and Compliance Gaining.* New York: Allyn and Bacon, 2004.

Gilovich, Thomas, Dale Griffin, and Daniel Kahneman eds. *Heuristics and Biases: The Psychology of Intuitive Judgment.* Cambridge, MA: Cambridge University Press, 2002.

Gitomer, Jeffrey. *The Sales Bible: The Ultimate Sales Resource.* New York: William Morrow, 1994.

Gregory, W.L., R. B. Cialdini, and K.M. Carpenter. "Self-Relevant Scenarios as Mediators of Likelihood Estimates and Compliance: Does Imaging Make It So? *Journal of Personality and Social Psychology,* 43 (1982): 89–99.

Hamer, Dean. *Living with Our Genes: Why They Matter More Than You Think.* New York: Doubleday, 1998.

Hogan, Kevin. *Irresistible Attraction: Secrets of Personal Magnetism.* Eagan, MN: Network 3000 Publishing, 2001.

Hogan, Kevin. *Science of Influence.* (CD Program) Eagan, MN: Network 3000 Publishing, 2004.

Hogan, Kevin. *The Psychology of Persuasion: How to Persuade Others to Your Way of Thinking.* Gretna, LA: Pelican Publishing, 1996.

Hogan, Kevin. *Through the Open Door: Secrets of Self Hypnosis.* Gretna, LA: Pelican Publishing, 2000.

Johnson, Kerry L. *Sales Magic: Revolutionary New Techniques That Will Double Your Sales Volume in 21 Days.* New York: William Morrow, 1994.

Johnson, Kerry L. *Subliminal Selling Skills.* New York: AMACOM, 1988.

Kahneman, Daniel, and Amos Tversky. *Choices, Values and Frames.* New York: Russell Sage Foundation, 2000.

Kahneman, Daniel, and Amos Tversky. "Loss Aversion in Riskless Choice: A Reference-Dependent Model." *Quarterly Journal of Economics* (1991).

Kennedy, Daniel S. *The Ultimate Sales Letter.* Holbrook, MA: Bob Adams, 1990.

Kent, Robert Warren. *The Art of Persuasion.* Surfside, FL: Lee Institute, 1963.

Knapp, Mark, and Judy Hall. *Nonverbal Communication in Human Interaction.* 3rd Ed. Fort Worth, TX: Harcourt Brace College Publications, 1992.

Knight, Sue. *NLP at Work: The Difference That Makes a Difference in Business.* Sonoma, CA: Nicholas Brealey Publishing, 1995.

Kostere, Kim. *Get the Results You Want: A Systematic Approach to NLP.* Portland, OR: Metamorphous Press, 1989.

Lavington, Camille, with Stephanie Losee. *You've Only Got Three Seconds: How to Make the Right Impression in Your Business and Social Life.* New York: Doubleday, 1997.

Lewis, David. *The Secret Language of Success: Using Body Language to Get What You Want.* New York: Carroll & Graf, 1990.

Linden, Anne, with Kathrin Perutz. *Mindworks: Unlock the Promise Within— NLP Tools for Building a Better Life.* Kansas City, MO: Andrews McMeel Publishing, 1997.

Lord, L. Ross, and M. R. Lepper. "Biased Assimilation and Attitude Polarization: The Effects of Prior Theories on Subsequently Conscious Evidence." (1979).

Mehrabian, Albert. *Silent Messages: Implicit Communication of Emotions and Attitudes.* Belmost, CA: Wadsworth, 1981.

Moine, Donald J., and John H. Herd. *Modern Persuasion Strategies: The Hidden Advantage in Selling.* Englewood Cliffs, NJ: Prentice-Hall, 1984.

Moine, Donald J., and Kenneth Lloyd. *Unlimited Selling Power: How to Master Hypnotic Selling Skills.* Englewood Cliffs, NJ: Prentice-Hall, 1990.

Myers, David G. *Intuition: Its Powers and Perils.* New Haven, CT: Yale University Press, 2003.

O'Keefe, Daniel J. *Persuasion: Theory and Research.* Thousand Oaks, CA: Sage Publications, 2003

Overstreet, H. A. *Influencing Human Behavior.* New York: W.W. Norton, 1925.

Patton, Forrest H. *Force of Persuasion: Dynamic Techniques for Influencing People.* Englewood Cliffs, NJ: Prentice-Hall, 1986.

Peoples, David. *Selling to the Top.* New York: John Wiley & Sons, 1993.

Perloff, Richard. *The Dynamics of Persuasion.* Hillside, NJ: Lawrence Erlbaum Associates, 1993.

Petty, R., and P. Brinol. "Nodding or Shaking Your Head May Even Influence Your Own Thoughts." *Journal of Personality and Social Psychology* (2003).

Piirto, Rebecca. *Beyond Mind Games: The Marketing Power of Psychographics.* Ithaca, NY: American Demographic Books, 1991.

Plous, Scott, *The Psychology of Judgment and Decision Making.* New York: McGraw-Hill, 1993.

Qubein, Nido. *Professional Selling Techniques: Strategies and Tactics to Boost Your Selling Skills and Build Your Career.* Rockville Centre, NY: Farnsworth Publishing Co., 1983.

Richardson, Jerry. *The Magic of Rapport.* Capitola, CA: Meta Publications, 1988.

Robbins, Anthony. *Unlimited Power.* New York: Fawcett, 1987.

Robertson, James E. *Sales the Mind's Eye: What They Didn't Teach You in Sales Training.* Portland, OR: Metamorphous Press, 1990.

Sadovsky, Marvin C., and Jon Caswell. *Selling the Way Your Customer Buys: Understand Your Prospects' Unspoken Needs & Close Every Sale.* New York: AMACOM, 1996.

Sherman, S.J., M.T. Crawford, and A. R. McConnell. "Looking Ahead as a Technique to Reduce Resistance to Persuasive Attempts." In *Resistance and Persuasion*, Eric S. Knowles and Jay A. Linn, eds. Mahwah, NJ: Lawrence Erlbaum Associates, 2004.

Slusher, M., and C. A. Anderson. "Using Casual Persuasive Arguments to Change Beliefs and Teach New Information: Mediating Role of Explanation Availability and Evaluation Bias in the Acceptance of Knowledge." *Journal of Educational Psychology* 88 (1996).

Sutherland, Stuart. *Irrationality: Why We Don't Think Straight.* Piscataway, NJ: Rutgers University Press, 1992.

Thaler, Richard. *The Winner's Curse: Paradoxes and Anomalies of Economic Life.* Princeton, NJ: Princeton University Press, 1992.

Thompson, George J., and Jerry B. Jenkins. *Verbal Judo: The Gentle Art of Persuasion.* New York: William Morrow, 1993.

Tracy, Brian. *Advanced Selling Strategies: The Proven System of Sales Ideas, Methods, and Techniques Used by Top Salespeople Everywhere.* New York: Fireside, 1995.

Vitale, Joe. *The Seven Lost Secrets of Success.* Houston: VistaTron, 1994.

Wegner, Daniel. *The Illusion of Conscious Will.* Cambridge, MA: Bradford Books, MIT Press, 2002.

Wegner D. M., and R. Erber. "Thought Suppression." *Annual Review of Psychology* (1992): 51–59.

Willingham, Ron. *The Best Seller: The New Psychology of Selling and Persuading People.* Englewood Cliffs, NJ: Prentice-Hall, 1984

Wilson, Timothy D. *Strangers to Ourselves: Discovering the Adaptive Unconscious.* Cambridge, MA: Belknap Press of Harvard University, 2002.

Witte, K., and M. Allen. "A Meta Analysis of Fear Appeals: Implications for Effective Public Health Campaigns." *Health, Education and Behavior* 27 (2000): 591-615.

Zimbardo, Philip G. *The Psychology of Attitude Change and Social Influence.* New York: McGraw-Hill. 1991.

Index

NEED A SPEAKER?

Both Kevin Hogan and James Speakman are dynamic speakers who involve and excite their audiences. With a passion for sharing powerful knowledge with people who will commit to its ethical use, both Kevin and James are ready to visit your company and conduct the kind of in-person training that only the live experience of their completely unique training can provide.

Kevin Hogan has spoken throughout the world from Sydney, Australia to Warsaw, Poland. Call Kevin personally at (612) 616-0732. Also, be sure to visit www.kevinhogan.com for more information on the power of persuasion. While visiting, be sure to sign up for *Coffee with Kevin Hogan*, a weekly e-newsletter that brings you a fresh piece of news every Monday morning regarding how to more successfully persuade and influence those you live and work with. In addition, you'll find dozens of free articles, plus the absolute best, most cutting edge audio and video programs centered on the latest research in this exciting and ever-changing field.

James Speakman has intensely studied the field of persuasion and delivers the live content in a powerfully persuasive way. He has shared these secrets with such power, energy, and involvement that participants leave with action plans that produce outstanding success. Find out more about James at www.jimspeakman.com. Be sure to sign up for the free e-newsletter as well.

Call or write Kevin or James today. Every passing day represents opportunities missed. Just imagine how much more successful you could be right now, if you would have already made the call, had the live training, and really put it all into use. Can you really afford to let another day go by?